FROM CYCLECAR TO MICROCAR

The story of the Cyclecar Movement

A National Motor Museum Trust book
by
Michael Worthington-Williams

Beaulieu Books

First Published in 1981

ISBN 0901564 540

© National Motor Museum Trust

Published by
DALTON WATSON LTD.
76 Wardour Street, London W1V 4AN
in association with
THE NATIONAL MOTOR MUSEUM TRUST

Printed in England by The Lavenham Press Ltd.

The light weight and narrow track of the cyclecar frequently enabled followers of the "New Motoring" to take them where larger cars could not follow. This led to a "go anywhere, do anything" legend which, apocryphal though it may have been, was seized upon and promoted by enthusiastic advocates of the cyclecar. This German artist obviously sees the 1920 cyclecar as something akin to a mountain goat, but the Wagnerian overtones are typical of the country and period.

Contents

Acknowledgment

The Author would like to acknowledge the kind assistance of all those involved in the preparation of this book, and in particular the following for their encouragement and interest, and for the loan of photographs and reference sources:-

Bill Boddy
Co-operative Wholesale Society
The late Bob Dicker
David Filsell
The late Michael Frostick
G N Georgano
David Hales
Tim Harding
Alistair Innes-Dick
IPC Business Press Ltd
Torleif Lindtveit (Norsk Teknisk Museum)
Lucien Lorreille
Mrs Grace Loveday
A Marshall (Surrey Micro-Car Collection)
Marshall, Harris & Baldwin
Keith Marvin
National Motor Museum
G Marshall Naul
Serge Pozzoli
Peter Roberts
Michael Sedgwick
The late Jack Shillan
The Reverend L C Stead
Richard Storey
Alvaro Casal Tatlock
David Thirlby
Veteran Car Club of Great Britain
Vintage Sports Car Club
(Light Car and Edwardian Section)
Michael Ware
Stan K Yost

Bibliography

The Motor (London)
Motor (Gutav Braunbeck, Berlin)
The Cyclecar (Temple Press)
The Light Car & Cyclecar (Temple Press)
The Light Car for Men and Women (Iliffe)
Old Motor (1st series)
Veteran & Vintage Magazine (Pioneer Publications)
The Upper Hudson Valley Automobilist (A.U.H.V.)
Floyd Clymer's Historical Motor Scrapbooks (Floyd Clymer)
From Brooklands to Goodwood (Foulis)
The Complete Encyclopaedia of Motor Cars (Ebury Press)
Continental Sports Cars (Foulis)
British Sports Cars (Floyd Clymer)
The History and Development of Light Cars (H.M.S.O.)
Light Cars and Cyclecars (Temple Press)
The World's Automobiles (Temple Press)
Historia del Automovil en Espana (Ediciones Ceac)
French Vintage Cars (Batsford/Autosport)
Deutsche Kleinwagen (Bleicher Motorbuch)
Danske Biler (Hassing)
Voitures Suisses (Edita, S.A.)
Cars of Canada (McLelland and Stewart)
The Book of the Motor Car (Caxton Publishing)
Racing Voiturettes (Motor Racing Publications)
The History of Brooklands Motor Course (Grenville Publishing)
Lost Causes of Motoring (Cassell)
Vintage Motor Car Pocketbook (Batsford)
The Motor Car 1946-56 (Batsford)

Introduction

Back in July 1965, in the late lamented *Veteran and Vintage* magazine, that controversial and influential journalist William Boddy of *Motor Sport* wrote an article entitled "The Greatest Lost Cause of All". Its subject was the cyclecar, in its original 1910-1925 guise, and in conclusion he said: "Few true cyclecars have survived, for they were crude when born, and quickly decayed. Yet a book could be written about this particular, rather forlorn, "lost cause", which was reared amid scenes of great enthusiasm, yet never had the backbone or stamina necessary for survival".

Not a few of Bill's excellent ideas and writings have proved the inspiration for worthwhile projects – take the Brooklands Society as an example – and yet, no-one has taken up the cyclecar challenge in the intervening years. This, then, is an attempt to fill that void and to take it further; to explore the development of the cyclecar and its derivatives throughout the Twentieth Century, through the medium of contemporary photographs – an illustrated history, in fact.

I am, of course, deeply conscious of the book's limitations, and for those whose appetites are whetted, I can heartily recommend Rodney Walkerley's classic history of the British Automobile Racing Club *Brooklands to Goodwood,* whilst there is nothing like a browse through bound copies of *Light Car and Cyclecar* at the National Motor Museum Library at Beaulieu for recapturing the essence of the period.

I must take issue with Bill Boddy, however, on the question of his definition of the cyclecar as "the greatest lost cause of all". I think that history will show that, just as cyclecars and minicars have played an almost continuous descant to the tune called by the orthodox light car, those roles might very well be reversed in the years to come.

Michael Worthington-Williams

THE TELESCOPIC CYCLECAR.

Prompted by a paragraph in a recent issue of "The Cyclecar" which referred to a collapsible machine designed :: :: :: by a reader. There are undoubtedly possibilities in the development of the idea. :: :: ::

Cartoons from The Cyclecar *January 22nd 1913*

Little Tommy (to his mother, who has just bought him a toy crocodile, as a Carden monocar passes at speed) :
"There's a real live one, mummy, on the road!"

AFTER BROOKLANDS. A DREAM OF THE FUTURE.

Chapter One

Quads, Trimos and Forecars

In the process of evolution, extinction, so we are told, is the rule rather than the exception, and in some respects the same is true of the motor car. Just as the multi-litred, chain-driven behemoths of the Edwardian period may be likened to the Brontosaurus, so were there lesser species which flourished for a period and then, having reached the peak of their development and unable to progress further or adapt to changing circumstances, withered and died away. The Victorian fore-car and its derivatives perhaps falls into this category.

Whatever else he may have been guilty of – and he was certainly no angel – Edward Joel Pennington may be credited with the popularisation of the forecar, or tri-car, in 1899, but it was his partner in crime, Harry J Lawson, whose Lawson Motor Wheel appeared in the same year, who may truthfully be said to have foreshadowed the cyclecars of the future. Of course, there were others – many of them unrecorded and unsung – who contributed ideas and ephemeral contrivances to the general evolutionary trend, but it was Pennington's rather than Lawson's ideas which shaped the following ten years or so of three wheeler development.

His forecar was built for him by Humber – a company in which both he and Lawson had financial interests – and consisted of a motorised bicycle, the engine of which (in the prototype at least) was located on an outrigger aft of the rear wheel, and the front wheel of which was replaced by a bath chair arrangement supported by two wheels, one on either side. The chair and front wheels were mounted on a steering head which permitted them to be steered by means of handlebars attached to the rear of the chair, in which sat the luckless passenger, fully exposed to the elements, road dust and the first available accident.

Thus located, with his (or more often, her) back to the conductor and with the wind rushing past, the passenger was effectively prevented from communicating with his companion, who in turn had his work cut out in steering the contraption, seeing the hazards ahead obscured by the passenger, and sitting astride (in most production models) a hot, noisy and recalcitrant engine.

This inherently unsociable arrangement was, believe it or not, designed to improve the sociability of the motorcycle and motor tricycle, the latter having been popularised by De Dion Bouton and widely copied, since its introduction in 1895. Whilst Pennington's device was not commercially successful, the idea was revived by J Van Hooydonk of Phoenix in 1903, became widely accepted, and was copied by Lagonda, Riley, Rover, Quadrant and many other makers.

Thus commenced the age of the forecar, and bearing in mind its uncivilised specification, the wretched device enjoyed an unusually long period of public acceptance. By 1905, however, Basil Crump was moved to write in *The Motor Yearbook:* "The development of the tricar during the past year has been considerable, but seems unlikely to be carried much further on the present lines . . . it has become practically a fast and light three-wheeled car. The most elaborate models are even more expensive than some of the cheaper two-seated cars, and nearly as heavy."

In fact, the usefulness of the forecar was drawing to a close, but it was not the light voiturette which ensured its demise. The introduction of the Liberty Sociable attachment in 1903 – one of the first motorcycle sidecar combination outfits – achieved what all motorcyclists had been aiming for: a truly sociable machine in which the fair sex could be carried in reasonable comfort side by side with the conductor, and in a position in which conversation (or sign language at least) could be carried on. From that time on, the story of the forecar was one of decline, albeit very gradual, and by 1907 virtually all its original espousers were either out of business, or making straightforward cars or motorcycles.

And so the initial chapter closed. Despite an editorial attempt by *The Motor Trader* in 1912, under an article entitled "The Antiquity of the Cycle-car", to link these early machines and some light voiturettes with the pure cyclecar (an exercise which smacks of the Mormon church baptising posthumously the dead of another religion into its own), there was no real connection, and very few vehicles – notably the A.C. Sociable and the Chater-Lea Carette – straddled contentiously the two eras.

It is perhaps true to say that the cyclecar is almost as old as the motor industry itself, and it is fitting, therefore, that one of its earliest manifestations should have been the product of a family whose first road vehicles – albeit steam powered – appeared in 1873. These first vehicles were built by bell founder Amédée Bollée of Le Mans, who continued to manufacture cars under his own name until 1922, but his son Léon Bollée concentrated his attention on really small petrol driven cars. When first announced in 1895, his tandem-seated "voiturette" three-wheeler boasted a 3 hp horizontal air-cooled 650 cc engine, hot tube ignition, three forward speeds and belt final drive. In this form it proved indecently fast, outstripping other petrol cars on the road, but of uncertain reliability. Charles McRobie Turrell, one-time secretary to the notorious H. J. Lawson, whose Humber works at Ford Street, Coventry, built this 1897 example under licence, opened his own works at Parkside and took over manufacture under the name Coventry Motette. Production ceased in 1899, both in France and England.

Although popularised by J. Van Hooydonk of Phoenix from 1903 onwards, the three-wheeled forecar was, in fact, first propounded in Britain by Humber in 1899, they having previously built the Léon Bollée under licence. Their own version is attributed to Edward Joel Pennington, and in keeping with that gentleman's idiosyncrasies of design wore its engine aft of the rear wheel on an outrigger. This circa 1904 Humber watercooled version conforms to the Van Hooydonk conception and persisted until 1905.

From the tri-car it was but a simple step to the motor quadricycle, and the Royal Enfield – a product of the Enfield Cycle Co. of Redditch in Worcester – was typical of several to appear around the turn of the century. Dating from circa 1901, this example is powered (as were all the Royal Enfield models) by a De Dion Bouton engine which was available in both 2¾ hp and 3½ hp guise. The driver still sat upon a bicycle-type saddle.

One of the lightest cars offered at the turn of the century was the Victoria Combination or Parisienne. It was powered by a 2¾ hp De Dion Bouton or 3½ hp Aster single-cylinder engine mounted over the front axle and driving the front wheels. The whole drive unit, engine, axle and wheels turned with the steering, a crudity generally out of favour by 1900, though the system is still found in 1980 on another French car, the Flipper (see page 108). Despite its flimsy appearance, the Victoria Combination was entered in long-distance trials, and one averaged 18 mph over a 150 mile route without an involuntary stop. More than 400 were made between 1899 and 1903.

Bearing in mind the somewhat maverick character which the cyclecar was to assume during the height of its popularity between 1910 and 1914, it is perhaps apposite that both H. J. Lawson and E. J. Pennington should have had a hand in the design of its precursors. This Lawson Motor Wheel was built for Lawson by A. W. Dougill & Co. at their premises at 36 Great George Street, Leeds in 1899 as a self-contained power unit. Consisting of road wheel, brake and fuel tank, it was adapted to fit any two wheeled horse drawn vehicle. It bore a remarkable likeness to the later Cyklon and anticipated the Smith Motor Wheel. The ladies are by no means in motoring gear of the period, and one may assume that they did not travel far in this smart attire.

Like Royal Enfield, the Alldays & Onions Pneumatic Engineering Co. (an old established Birmingham company dating – as bellows manufacturers – from 1650) relied on a De Dion engine for their 4 hp Traveller introduced in 1898 as their first essay into car production. Made in private and commercial forms, it went one better than the Enfield in that wheel steering was employed, and the driver enjoyed a properly upholstered seat – albeit the rear of the vehicle was unsprung. This model was current until 1904.

The popularity of the high speed De Dion Bouton engine with English manufacturers of light voiturette-type vehicles was largely due to the outstanding success of the De Dion Bouton tricycle, the patent rights for which had been acquired by H. J. Lawson. His New Beeston Cycle & Motor Co. was formed primarily to build copies in Coventry, and his re-formed Motor Manufacturing Co., under the direction of ex-L.B.S.C.R. engineer George Iden, also built them as M.M.C.'s. Unfortunately expensive "improvements", which included the scrapping of Georges Bouton's electric ignition in favour of hot tube, ensured the failure of Lawson's most promising enterprise. This is a "genuine" De Dion tricycle of 1900, wearing interesting stone catchers behind the rear tyres.

Typical of the many French versions of the tri-car or forecar which flourished until about 1907/8, the Contal (or Mototri-Contal) was built at 64 Avenue de la Grande Armée in Paris, and lasted only from 1905 until 1908. A 6 hp watercooled affair, it is seen here with its driver Rivière at the 1905 Paris Concours de Tri-cars. Its main claim to fame, however, was Contal et Cie's entry in the 1907 Pekin to Paris race. Out of a total of twenty-five entrants, it, together with two De Dions, a Spyker and Prince Scipione Borghese's Itala actually started on this epic event. Alas, it was much too frail for the terrain, and was abandoned in the Gobi Desert.

Before the Great War, and even during the twenties, America's rural road system lagged far behind her European counterparts and in many areas her unmade roads were impassable in winter. Extremely light vehicles like the Massachusetts-built Waltham Orient Buckboard were, therefore, in the minority and it is significant that the Waltham Mfg. Co. commenced their operations with motor tricycles powered by De Dion engines. Of the simplest design, the Buckboard was tiller steered and unsprung, its 4 hp aircooled engine geared direct to the rear axle with but one speed. It sold in Britain for £94 10s.0d. complete.

The little German Cyklon hailed from Berlin and, like the better-known Phänomobil, carried its engine above the single front wheel, which it drove by chain. Introduced in three wheeled form at the 1902 Leipzig Motor Show, it was tiller steered and powered by a single cylinder air-cooled 450 cc engine. From 1904 it was known as the Cyklonette, later acquired a twin cylinder 1290 cc engine and four seats and was also built as a van. It continued in basically unaltered form until 1922, by which time the company was owned by coachbuilders Schapiro. Conventional cars were thereafter built under the Cyklon Schebera names.

Chater-Lea were better known for their motor cycles and components, but from 1907 until 1922 they dabbled with a variety of light vehicles and cyclecars. Of these, the Carette, introduced in 1907 and current into 1908, was interesting in that the engine – a 6 hp Vee-twin aircooled Sarolea – was mounted amidships on the offside of the vehicle, with final drive to one rear wheel only by Hans Renold chain. This specification, allied to the extremely low price of 95 guineas, spelt cyclecar in all but name. Experiments continued until 1913, when a conventional 8 hp shaft driven car appeared.

Bridging the gap between the forecar and the cyclecar proper, the O.T.A.V. (Officine Turkheimer Automobili e Velocipedi) from Milan flourished from 1905 until 1908 in the voiturette class. Despite its spartan specification – aircooled single cycle 5½ hp engine, two-speed epicyclic gearing and belt drive – it acquitted itself well, one example covering 388 miles in 19 hours in the Essex Motor Club York Run. At 95 guineas, it competed directly with the Chater-Lea Carette. The company was associated with Giovanni Geirano's Turin based Junior concern, which also built voiturettes

Outwardly resembling the later L.A.D. and Harper Runabout by virtue of the fact that its engine was worn on the offside amidships, the Unecar was one of the very earliest British monocars to appear at the commencement of the true cyclecar era and was announced in August 1910. Designed by W. W. Bannister of Maidstone, and, like many early cyclecars, first described in the motorcycle rather than the motorcar press, the machine was belt driven, tiller steered, tubular framed and resembled an invalid carriage.

The Wolverhampton-built Wolf Motette, a product of the Wearwell Motor Carriage Company, was typical of the lighter belt-driven forecars of 2¾ hp – 3¼ hp popular during the early Edwardian period and of the type advocated in 1907 by the inimitable "Ixion" of The Motor Cycle. Unfortunately, by that date tricars and forecars were developing a tendency towards large engines of 6 hp upwards and increased weight all round, with the result that eventually some of them were heavier than conventional four seater cars – and more expensive – and the type had thus outgrown its usefulness. The need for sociability was latterly catered for by the motorcycle and sidecar combination.

Chapter Two

Revolution: The Wire, Bobbin and Fibre Board Brigade

In retrospect, the Cyclecar Movement, or New Motoring, contained all the elements of a radical political party. Revolutionary both in its ideas and its ideology, fervent in its adherents who were impervious either to criticism or vicissitude, it was anti-establishment and even left-wing. And yet it was always sociable in its aims rather than socialist, and more akin in many ways to a philosophy. For this it could largely either thank or blame *The Light Car & Cyclecar* which, having harnessed the latent enthusiasm of the "New Motorists", proceeded to exert a proprietorial influence over the whole cyclecar movement.

Not only did its doctrines advocate a purity and simplicity in the designs of the cyclecar itself, but to an extent a puritanism and simplicity in the way cyclecarists lived their lives. In the beginning, at least, the accent was upon the romance of the open road, the family outing in the healthy open air, the picnic, the harmless fun of it all. There was something vaguely moral about it, a thought underlined by the fact that, despite the speeding, the noise, and the snoots cocked at "the three gloomy gentlemen in charge of a measured furlong", the first run of The Cyclecar Club on 7th December 1912 finished up at the Rev. E. P. Greenhill's home at Walton-on-the-Hill for tea.

By 1913, and with the smack of Temperance fervour, *The Cyclecar* was propounding its ideas for "The Simple Life Hotel", where the fare was to be plain but good, the charges moderate, and the rooms clean and comfortable. Owners of 40/50 hp Rolls-Royces or "gilded youths driving snorting Mercs" would most definitely not be catered for, but Followers of the New Motoring (sic) on a modest cyclecar tour would be made welcome with a 5/-d six-course dinner and a 3/6d lunch!

So what *was* the cyclecar, in what ways was it new, and why is it necessary to deal with it in isolation? We have already seen that the tri-car in its original form put on weight, became expensive and was in many ways impractical. By 1909, the demand for a small, ultra-light vehicle bridging the gap between the motorcycle combination and the motor car proper, although latent, was acute, and whilst in retrospect this "gap in the market" is glaringly apparent, none of the established manufacturers lifted a finger to satisfy it. Quite why this should have been is difficult to fathom; possibly the memory of the only recently-extinct tri-car was still too painful, but whatever the reason, it was from outside the existing motor industry that the answer was to come. Perhaps the buying public were at fault too, for although they wanted a replacement for the tri-car, they had no idea what form it should take.

When the solution was found – in the period 1909/1910 – it followed virtually the same formula in Britain, France and the United States. Quite how this spontaneous fruition of ideas came about is something of a mystery, since so far as we know none of the individuals involved had any contact with, or knowledge of, one another. Certainly, however, the ingredients were the same even if the recipe was slightly different, and all had one thing in common – ultra-light weight allied to a powerful engine of motorcycle derivation, or, as some put it, combining the worst features of the motorcycle with the more depressing aspects of the motorcar!

As with the motor car itself, controversy rages as to who built the first cyclecar. The argument is largely academic, however, since no more than a matter of months could possibly have separated the efforts of the original advocates, and one of the first was undoubtedly Morgan. It is, perhaps, as a result of its origins that the cyclecar breed engendered a purity and naivete of purpose, and a joie de vivre which was to express itself in the open air, sporting events and competitions, for it was the product of the very young.

The first Morgan was constructed in the workshops of Malvern College, Worcestershire, and the eventual production was financed with the assistance of H. F. S. Morgan's father, the Reverend Prebendiary H. George Morgan. Similarly, the constructors of the 3½hp Quentin-engined Bedelia in Paris, Henri Bourbeau and Robert Devaux, were both only eighteen when the prototype was conceived in 1910, and both received parental financial assistance. The G.N., another 1910 arrival, was constructed by H. R. "Ron" Godfrey and Archie Frazer-Nash in the stable of Nash's mother's home, The Elms at Hendon, and albeit reluctantly, she financed the first one.

Thus launched, and despite the inauspicious

REVOLUTION: THE WIRE, BOBBIN AND FIBRE BOARD BRIGADE

circumstance of its conception, the cyclecar, as propounded by these early experimenters, was taken up enthusiastically by the motor-cycling press, by the public, and by other would-be constructors.

In 1912, cyclecars were included in the Cycle and Motor Cycle Show at Olympia, but it was possibly W. G. McMinnies, editor of the Temple Press journal *Motor Cycling,* who gave the "movement" its greatest boost. Having seen Bourbeau in a prototype Bedelia in Paris in 1910, he became an immediate convert, and on his return to London eventually persuaded his boss Arthur Armstrong and his employers that a need existed for a new journal "to focus and foster the enthusiasm that was bound to flare up when these machines begin to come on to the market at prices well under £100". The result was *The Cyclecar.* Launched on 27th November 1912 under the editorship of Samuel Dangerfield it provided 64 editorial pages (and no less than 84 pages of advertising) for the princely sum of one penny (pre-decimal), and in two printings it sold a record 100,000 copies.

The cyclecar having arrived, it had to be catered for. Because it was fast, cheap and somewhat rakish in appearance, it attracted not only disaffected motorcyclists and those impecunious types with no previous motoring experience (hence "New" motoring), but also those of a sporting persuasion for whom, hitherto, speed could be obtained only at considerable expense. Not only did the cyclecar prove equal in performance to its very much larger and expensive cousins, it frequently displayed an ability to wipe the floor with cars costing ten times as much — to the chagrin of owners of vehicles in the latter class.

The Auto-Cycle Union (the motorcycle branch of the R.A.C.) decided that such sporting potential was too good to be lost to the R.A.C., especially with its promise of a flood of new membership fees, and the new motorists were therefore taken under its wing. It is interesting that the term "cyclecar" was coined by Col. Lindsay Lloyd, Clerk of the Course at Brooklands, and an A.-C.U. member, at the meeting at which this decision was taken, and its subsequent universal adoption may in part be attributed to him.

Ignoring the fact that the cyclecar was regarded with undisguised hostility by many motorcyclists, and there was no love lost between the remainder, the A.-C.U. applied to the ruling body for motor sport, the *Federation Internationale des Clubs Moto-cyclistes* in Paris, for approval of a cyclecar definition. By the time that *The Cyclecar* was achieving record sales, the following definition had been promulgated at international level:

Group 1. Large Class
Maximum weight 772lb (just under 7-cwt)
Maximum engine capacity 1,100cc
(International Class G)

Group 2. Small Class
Maximum weight 660lb (just under 6cwt);
Minimum 330lb.
Maximum engine capacity 750cc
(International Class H)

The formation of The Cyclecar Club at the Holborn Restaurant, London on 30th October 1912 was an inevitably logical step, the credit for which goes to Ernest Perman (appropriately of Temple Press). The inaugural meeting was chaired by Arthur Armstrong of *Motor Cycling* and others present included W. G. McMinnies, H. R. Godfrey, Osmond Hill and Frank "Hippopo" Thomas. The Club's first run to the Wisley Hut Hotel near Esher took place on 7th December 1912.

Not to be outdone, France formed its own club, Le Cyclecar Club de France, with its own journal *Cyclecars, Motos et Voitures,* and it was not long before the movement was well-served with journals. From America came *The American Cyclecar,* for although the United States was a little slow off the mark to develop interest in the cyclecar, well over 100 manufacturers were eventually established and by March 1914 there was widespread talk in Europe of an "American Invasion" of cheap vehicles. One English journal devoted a double page spread to a cartoon in which American cyclecars were depicted as an Armada approaching European shores.

In the event, the invasion never took place, although a number of American makes were imported with limited success. The fact is, the cyclecar did not "catch on" in the U.S. for a variety of reasons. Quite apart from the fact that the Model T Ford, and other full-sized cars like it, could be purchased very cheaply there, fuel was plentiful and low-priced — which did not encourage engines of cyclecar

REVOLUTION: THE WIRE, BOBBIN AND FIBRE BOARD BRIGADE

size – and roads outside cities and towns were incredibly bad. The war in Europe, and America's entry into it in 1917, sealed the fate of the American cyclecar, and like the Detroit-built Dodo – one of the first U.S. makes – it became extinct not long after the war.

The Autocar tried to cash in on the boom with *The Light Car for Men and Women,* and a furious row developed when *The Cyclecar* changed its name to *The Light Car and Cyclecar* only a few months later. Thus it stayed however until, in 1933, the title was shortened to *The Light Car,* and Iliffe's journal proved short-lived. But the sport went from strength to strength. The first cyclecar race was held at Brooklands in 1913, and all over the country owners competed in hill climbs, trials and sprints, all of which were enthusiastically reported.

In France, the classic Coupe de l'Auto had been handed over to the *voitures legères* and for a time there had been a real danger that, so far as racing was concerned, the real voiturette would become entirely neglected. In 1913, therefore, the Automobile Club de France Grand Prix at Amiens provided the opportunity for a 'revival'. This took the form of a race for cyclecars – a Cyclecar Grand Prix in fact – and was run on 13th July, the day following the main Grand Prix.

It included motorcycles and sidecars, and was won by McMinnies, but since the organisers classified three wheelers as motorcycles, his Morgan was forced to concede the laurels to a French Bedelia – a decision which caused some ire in the Morgan camp.

Three weeks later, on 4th August, the cyclecars met again in an event designed to open the festivities preceding the Grand Prix de France at Le Mans, and whilst Morgans were understandably conspicuous by their absence, the event was interesting in that Peugeot entered three Bébés. Although they managed 3rd, 5th and 6th places, they were beaten by a cyclecar – the Ronteix – at an average of 46.9mph.

The outbreak of war on 4th August 1914 (the day after *The Light Car and Cyclecar* was published), whilst imposing restrictions on many manufacturers of larger vehicles whose sophisticated production facilities were required for war work, did not immediately prevent the continuation of construction of several makes of cyclecar. Because of the simplicty of its general design and the materials – wood, fibreboard and the like – associated with the chassis and bodywork, it could be, and frequently was, built in workshops which were unsuitable for the production of munitions, and its raw materials made no great inroads into the needs of the war effort.

Cyclecars which had been made by the larger car firms and motorcycle manufacturers were affected, however, and many did not reappear when hostilities ceased. The frugal French, with characteristic versatility and disregard for the safety of life and limb, pressed the Bedelia into service as a field ambulance, and even the British tried out the Scott Sociable as a mobile mounting for the Vickers machine gun before settling for Clyno, Matchless and Zenith combinations for their Motor Cycle Machine Gun Corps.

By 1917, however, the war which everyone had expected to be over by Christmas 1914 had eliminated virtually all the pre-war names from active production. Many of them had been one-man businesses for whom dreams of post-war production ended in a mud-filled Flanders trench – others lost for ever the *esprit de corps* which had pervaded the whole of the pre-war cyclecar "movement", and exchanged the gay comrades-in-adversity atmosphere which had then existed for a new grim brand of comradeship. Whatever happened after the war, things would never be quite the same again.

Archie Frazer-Nash first met H. R. "Ron" Godfrey in 1905 when both men were first year students in Mechanical Engineering at Finsbury. In December 1910 they built a Vee twin-engined belt driven "Quad" in the grounds of Nash's mother's house, The Elms at Hendon, which was written up in The Motorcycle *and by 1911 they were manufacturing G.N. cyclecars with their own Peugeot based Vee-twin i.o.e. engnes, and a variety of transmissions by belt and/or chain, at the rate of two a week.*
This is a rare three-seater model, made at the end of 1915.

Imitation is the sincerest form of flattery, and it is only to be expected that following their initial success, G.N. should have had to contend with plagiarists. The Sabella, built in Camden Town by Fritz Sabel (a near relative coincidentally, of that great early vehicle enthusiast, the late Peter Black of Keighley), was such a copy, although, in fairness, Sabel had been in the light car business since 1906, previously exhibiting at the Stanley Show in that year, and 1907. Shown here is Royal Flying Corps air ace McCudden (the passenger) in his Sabella during his period as an Air Mechanic at Farnborough. Note rear seat steering, necessitating the very long pipe to the horn.

The Sabella was also popular as a family car, however, and in 1913 Gilbert Bratchell (seen here with his wife and children) wrote in glowing terms of his 1912 model. Despite the tandem seating, the children were apparently easily accommodated – a total weight four up of 28 stone – and with this normal load the 8-10 hp J.A.P. engine (which drove a primary chain and final belt to the rear wheels) returned on average of 50 mpg. The year's running costs worked out at 1¹/sd. (pre-decimal) per mile. With no previous motorcycling experience and attracted to motoring by the cyclecar, Bratchell was typical of those "new motorists" from whom arose the term the "New Motoring".

It is generally accepted that the Paris-built Bedelia was the first of the really successful French cyclecars, and certainly it was one of the most popular and longest-lived. Taking its name from the phonetics BeeDee of the surnames of its designers Henri Bourbeau and Robert Devaux, and similar in appearance to the Billancourt-built Automobilette, it resembled a long wooden coffin on wheels. Power was provided by single cylinder or Vee twin aircooled engines of from 3½ hp to 10 hp driving the rear wheels through enormously long belts. The driver steered from the rear seat by a system of wires and bobbins to a crude centre pivot, while the passenger varied the tension of the belts with a lever, and (initially at least) shifted the belts from the high speed to the low speed pulley with a stick! This example was built for the 1913 Cyclecar Grand Prix.

The Adamson cyclecar was built by R. Barton Adamson & Co., well-known transport contractors of Enfield Highway, Middlesex, and in production form was a low built (by virtue of an underslung frame), good looking machine. Experimental vehicles, however, included an unconventional catamaran-type cyclecar with engine amidships and separate passenger compartments on either side. Production cars utilised twin cylinder watercooled Alpha engines, three speed gearboxes and belt final drive. Shown here is cyclecar advocate and well-known contributor to The Cyclecar, Dr. A. M. Low, A.C.G.I., D.Sc. (the cyclecarist's answer to Magnus Pike!) in his 1914 model.

More substantially built than many of its contemporaries, the Vox, although manufactured by Lloyd & Plaister in Wood Green, owed its engine design to the much earlier Shoreham-built Dolphin. Designed by Harry Ricardo, this was a Vee configuration, twin cylinder, watercooled two stroke with one working cylinder and one pumping cylinder with leaf spring inlet valve. About 50 were sold up until 1915, and with tubular chassis and shaft drive they were otherwise conventional.

Built from 1908 until 1914, the A.C. Sociable was a true missing link between the tricar and the cyclecar, and was equally popular during both eras. Designed by John Weller initially as a small parcel carrier ("Autocarrier" – hence A.C.) for wealthy West Norwood butcher John Portwine, it was made originally in West Norwood and from 1911 in Thames Ditton, where A.C. still flourish. Fitted with a single cylinder engine with mechanically operated inlet valve, two speed epicyclic gear, tiller steering and chain drive, they were good value at £92 10s.0d. This one, photographed in Wendover, Bucks. in 1913, is operated by a commercial traveller.

Between 1912 and 1913 the Premier Co. Ltd. produced two distinct types of cyclecar – the P.M.C. Motorette three wheeler with rear mounted 6 hp single cylinder engine and chain final drive, and the Premier (illustrated here crossing Charlecote Bridge over the River Avon near Stratford in February 1913). Not to be confused with the German Premier marketed by Braun-Premier at the same time, the latter model sold for 100 guineas, was powered by a 998 cc 50° Vee twin engine and employed a two speed and reverse gearbox and chain drive. Factories were maintained in both Birmingham and Coventry.

Originally located in Shepherd's Bush from 1912 until 1914 and initially known as the Lambert & West, the Warren-Lambert was one of the better cyclecars — a fact which, as with other successful cars of its kind, ensured that in post-war form it would grow into a fully fledged light sports car and lose its cyclecar image. Up until 1914 a watercooled Blumfield twin cylinder engine was employed, and all examples enjoyed shaft drive. Renowned for its hill climbing abilities, the marque conquered the notorious Nailsworth Ladder in the Cotswolds with ease, and is seen here in 1914 ascending the Booklands test hill "five-up". The designer, A. W. Lambert, took his bride Miss Elsie Warner on their honeymoon in the prototype.

Despite a proliferation of makes — well over a hundred — and massive fears of an "American Invasion" in Britain, the cyclecar never really caught on in the United States. Outside towns and cities roads were so bad that the average cyclecar would have rattled to pieces in no time, fuel was plentiful and the Model T Ford was cheap. Of all the U.S. makes, the Imp built by W. H. McIntyre of Auburn, Indiana (makers of the full sized McIntyre) most closely followed European practice and was one of the most successful. Utilising a large Vee twin engine mounted à-la-Morgan at the front of the car, the Imp boasted tandem seating, friction transmission and long belt drive. It cost US$375.00 and the single "Cyclops" headlamp was a trademark. Note the offset starting handle, linked to the crankshaft by chain.

Think of Bradford and you automatically think of Jowett, which, in twin cylinder form and as originally conceived, was, perhaps, a rugged link between the cyclecar and the light car. Other makes came from the same town, however, and in addition to the ephemeral Jewel built by John E. Wood for nearly twenty years in Bowland Street – initially a cyclecar – there was the Gilyard from Barkerend Road, made from 1912 to 1916. Of some sporting proclivity, and powered by a watercooled 8 hp twin cylinder Chater-Lea engine, it relied upon chain final drive and cost £100. Here, R.T. Cawthorne fields his Gilyard at Sutton Bank hill climb.

Despite its exotic name there is no reason to believe that the 1920 La Rapide, built in Southwest London, was either exotic or rapid. The cowling on the offside conceals the fact that the engine – an 8 p aircooled J.A.P. – was worn amidships mounted on two extended cross members, an unusual disposition shared by the post-war Gibbons. Power was transmitted by primary chain to a Sturmey-Archer three speed gearbox and thence by belt to the offside wheel only, thus (theoretically) dispensing with the need for a differential.

One of the beauties of the simplicity of the cyclecar is that it enabled almost anyone to become a manufacturer – almost anywhere. And if the venture was not the success that had been hoped, it was as inexpensive to stop manufacture as it had been to commence. No large factories, expensive machinery, staff to lay off or materials to dispose of. The Challenge cyclecar shown here was built by a Mr. Marcus at 9 Golders Green Crescent, N.W.4, immediately prior to the Great War and briefly, as the Marcus, in 1920. Aircooled, with central belt drive passing between the two seats, it cost just £100, and was designed by a Mr. Coult of Hendon.

It might be thought that the "kit" car was a phenomenon peculiar to the last twenty years of motorcar manufacture, but such is not the case. Because of its general simplicity of design and construction, the cyclecar particularly lent itself to the attentions of the "home builder", and several firms catered for the D.I.Y. motorist before the Great War. Among many who offered cyclecar components were the Hackney-based company of Hurlin & Co. who also built the Hurlincar light car and the Aviette cyclecar. The latter is illustrated in monocar form here with 4 hp J.A.P. single cyclinder engine, central pivot steering and chain-cum-belt drive – all for £55. Note the "garden fence" bodywork – a change from the kipper box and tea chest variety.

Harold E. Dew of Eynsford, Kent (seen here) may be numbered among the very earliest advocates of the single seater cyclecar or monocar. In September 1910 his "Whippet Spider" was reported in The Motor – a 2½ cwt tubular framed lightweight with aircooled 4½ hp J.A.P. engine and central belt drive from an adjustable pulley to the rear axle. Production models were called Dewcars and utilised Precision engines of 4½ hp and 8 hp in the monocar and two seater. Both were belt driven, but following a move to Ealing in 1914 the name was changed to Victor. Dew then popped up again in Clapham with the 8 hp Chater-Lea engined twin cylinder D-Ultra with friction transmission and chain final drive at £115. Production ceased in 1916. Note the prestine cleanliness of the engine and chain transmission to the countershaft.

The Buchet-engined Baby was the best-known
model of the C.I.D., the Dijon-based company
who had previously built the Cottereau car.
Offered between 1912 and 1914, the Baby
employed a single cylinder engine and four speed
friction transmission. Quite why this one should
be parked outside the London premises of the
Cummikar is rather a mystery. Cummikars were
also cyclecars but built by Ronteix, who employed
several Sizaire-Naudin features in their cars –
including transverse front springing similar to
that employed by the Baby. The firms may have
been connected.

J. F. Buckingham's engine works in Spon Street,
Coventry, originally offered single cylinder and
Vee twin engines to other manufacturers but in
1913 commenced manufacture of the Chota
cyclecar. In September 1913 the name was
changed, logically, to Buckingham and the cars
were offered with two forward speeds and belt
drive. Well constructed, light and fast,
Buckinghams were successful in pre-war
competition and one is seen here with J.F.
Buckingham at the wheel. After the war the
works transferred to the Alvis factory in
Holyhead Road, Coventry, and the car acquired
a conventional three speed box and bevel drive. It
had put on weight, however, and was not
popular. Production ceased in 1923.

The 1912 Eagle was, perhaps, more of a light car
than a cyclecar and although the 8/10 hp engine
was a Vee twin set transversely across the frame,
it was made in the works. Two models, both with
shaft drive, employed a tubular frame and (as
illustrated) a pressed steel frame respectively,
and the latter was virtually identical to the
Omnium offered (at the same price of £135) from
an anonymous Great Portland Street address.
Perhaps the Eagle's main claim to fame is that it
was built in the same Beverley Works at Barnes
which were later to see the birth of the
Beverley-Barnes luxury car. The car wears an
early example of a trade plate, A4 EMC. These
were issued to manufacturers, and the last
three letters presumably stand for
Eagle Motor Company

The Batley-built J.B.S. (named after its sponsors J. Bagshaw & Sons) appeared during the cyclecar boom in 1913 and initially employed an 8 hp Vee twin J.A.P. engine, albeit with watercooling and shaft drive. As evidenced by the illustrations, this diminutive unit was nevertheless sufficient to propel the J.B.S. up the more wicked gradients of its native Yorkshire but in 1915 four cylinder Blumfield and Dorman units were adopted and the J.B.S. became a fully fledged light car. The war halted production in 1915.

As we have seen, Humber were no strangers to light car production and it is, therefore, not surprising that following their forecars – and the watercooled 5 hp Humberette offered at 120 guineas from 1903 – they should take advantage of the cyclecar boom of 1912. Their Humberette cyclecar was a quality product reasonably priced at £120 (£15 extra for watercooling) and boasted a Vee twin aircooled 8 hp engine mounted transversely and in-unit with the three speed gearbox, shaft drive and full differential. It was to point the way to the post-war 8/18 light car.

The German three-wheeled Phänomobil followed the unorthodox but nevertheless successful design of the Cyklonette in that it wore its engine above the single front wheel, steered by tiller, and employed vertical chain drive. In continuous production from 1907 until at least 1927, and possibly a little later, the Phänomobil was an anachronism comparable, perhaps, with the British Trojan. Certainly its unorthodoxy could be offset by its reliability, economy and utility and it proved extremely popular. In two or four seater guise, it even appeared with coachbuilt saloon bodywork by Lond & Weigold of Berlin in 1922! Offered initially as a Vee or vertical twin, four cylinder engines of 1536cc were employed after 1912.

Throughout the history of the cyclecar there crop up the names of certain individuals – like Harold Dew – whose unorthodoxy is equalled only by their optimism; an optimism moreover which must have been infectious since they never seemed to be short of enthusiastic sponsors. Such a man was Marcel Violet who, later in his career, was to espouse the two stroke engine for many of his creations. The Violet-Bogey, the first cyclecar to be designed by him, was, however, an advanced machine with a twin cylinder 1100cc watercooled engine with large overhead inlet valves, friction disc primary drive and chain final drive to the differential-less rear axle. 22bhp at 2,400rpm ensured considerable success in pre-war competition. Here, Anthony refuels during the 1913 Cyclecar Grand Prix at Le Mans.

Like many American cyclecars the Trumbull from Bridgeport, Connecticut, employed a watercooled four cylinder engine of 1.7 litres – considerably larger than its European counterparts. Friction transmission and double chain drive were, however, cyclecar features, although shaft drive was eventually adopted. By the time this circa 1915 model was proudly shown by film star Lincoln Stedman to Ella Hall as his first car on the 23rd June 1927, the American cyclecar industry was long dead and even Henry's Lizzie was bowing out.

The Woods Mobilette was one of the earliest of the American cyclecars, the prototype being built in 1910 and was billed as "America's First Cyclecar". Experiments with air-cooled engines delayed production until 1914, however, by which time the war in Europe had commenced and the cyclecar boom was on the wane. Like the Adamson, the Woods Mobilette was underslung, production models boasting four cylinder watercooled engines (a typical American feature) and two speed gear boxes, seating being in tandem. By 1916 staggered side by side seating was offered, with electric lighting and starting as optional extra. America's entry into the war in 1917 heralded the marque's demise.

Just as many "lost causes" of the full-sized automobile industry rallied round one another to keep each other afloat, so did many cyclecar and light car firms maintain complicated links. The Deptford-built Duo (which incidentally featured on the front cover of the first issue of The Cyclecar in 1912) is an example. A conventional belt driven machine which shopped around extensively for engines during its two year life (Buckingham, Dorman, Chapuis-Dornier and Mathis were some used), the Duo was taken over by L. F. de Peyrecave (who built De P cars) and some 1913 offerings – like this one – were known as De P Duos.

As Bill Boddy once said, the cyclecar fever which commenced in 1910 had, by 1912, become a raging disease and by the Autumn of 1912 was an epidemic of startling proportions. So much so, that, like Humber, many established manufacturers began to look seriously at the cyclecar market. Among them were Swift of Coventry who, since 1900, had made a variety of voiturettes as well as larger, more substantial, cars. The result was their 1912 7 hp twin cylinder watercooled cyclecar, albeit with shaft drive. By 1914 it had acquired a pressed steel frame (shown here) in place of the original tubular chassis, all models being made by the Swift Cycle Co. subsidiary.

Bearing in mind the earliest cars of Alldays & Onions, it is perhaps understandable that they should field a cyclecar in 1913. The Alldays Midget was, however, more refined than most offerings, for although the 990 cc Vee twin engine was aircooled, a three speed gearbox and shaft drive were employed. An increase in price from £138 10s.0d. to £157 10s.0d. in 1914 heralded an 8-10 hp 1093 cc four cylinder watercooled version which took the model into the light car class, and by the outbreak of war the price had risen to £175.

Apart from Willys Overland Crossley at Heaton Chapel, very few makes of car emanated from Stockport, but among them was the Woodrow, which eked out a precarious existence in Wellington Road North between 1913 and 1915. Offered in air and watercooled form at £126 and £140 respectively with J.A.P. and Precision Vee twin 8 hp engines, the Woodrow enjoyed the luxury of a three speed gearbox and a full differential, although initially chain final drive was employed. Later models offered worm drive rear axle, and in sporting form with pointed radiator and streamlined body the car was capable of respectable performances. Note the liberally drilled chassis and isolated petrol tank of this stripped Brooklands model.

The Beacon was built initially at Hindhead, Surrey, at the Beacon Hill Motor Works in 1912, and from 1913 until 1914 at Liphook, Hampshire. Designed by Angus Maitland, who had previously designed the conventional Robinson & Hole car at Thames Ditton, Surrey, the make is chiefly remembered for an experimental propeller driven car (like the French Leyat) and the optional woven cane body on the ultra-light 6 cwt model. Prototypes used a J.A.P. Vee twin engine and chain or friction drive, but production models standardised on the French Griffon Vee twin aircooled 1090 cc engine and shaft drive to a rear axle-mounted three speed gearbox.

The Crouch Carette, built at Tower Gate Works, Cook Street, Coventry, was typical of that breed of cyclecar which achieved great popularity before the Great War but which "grew up" after the Armistice. Of more substantial construction than most, the Crouch carried its watercooled Vee twin Coventry-Simplex engine amidships and in this respect it resembled the snub-nosed appearance of the pre-war G.W.K. Three forward speeds, chain drive and full differential completed the specification. This 1915 example belongs to the Manx Motor Museum. Post-war cars, initially still twin cylindered, wore their engines at the front and adopted shaft drive, in which form they achieved some sporting success. In final form from 1923 with four cylinder Anzani engine the Crouch was a pure light car.

Pearsall-Warne Ltd. of Letchworth – home of the Phoenix in its declining years – hedged their bets between 1913 and 1915 by offering the Warne both as a light car and a cyclecar. The cyclecar was offered initially with J.A.P. (later in 1914 with Precision) Vee twin air-cooled engines and chain-cum-belt final drive via a system of expanding pulleys and dog clutches giving an infinitely variable gear ratio. The light car, weighing 1 cwt more at 7 cwt, utilised a watercooled version of the Precision Vee twin, three speed gearbox and shaft and bevel drive as illustrated here.

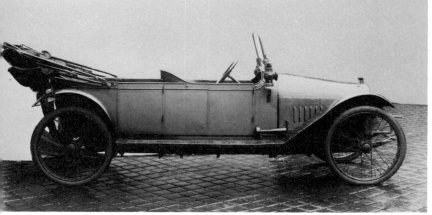

No fewer than three American makes rejoiced in the name of Twombly, and the third of these, introduced in 1913, was a cyclecar. Although the factory was in Nutley, New Jersey, the cars were built in Sharon, Pennsylvania, by the Driggs-Seabury Ordnance Corpn., who at various times were also responsible for the Sharon, Driggs, Driggs-Seabury cyclecar, Ritz cyclecar, and the Ohio-built Vulcan. Although offered with tandem seating and initially with a twin cylinder aircooled engine and friction drive, the Twombly inevitably acquired a four cylinder L head watercooled engine, three speeds and shaft drive, in which form it cost US$660.

Douglas were typical of the well established motorcycle firms who entered the cyclecar fray at its highest – Matchless, Ariel and B.S.A. all fielded light cars of varying sophistication into the twenties – and with a fair degree of success. Miss Addis-Price competed with a racing version at Brooklands and John Alcock (later Sir John Alcock) of aviation fame supplemented his Humber with a saloon version. Power was obtained from a large Williamson flat twin motorcycle engine (Williamson himself was related to the Douglas family by marriage) in both watercooled and aircooled form allied to friction disc transmission and worm final drive. Designed by Willie Douglas, the car project was approved by William Douglas Senr., seen here with his own coupé version at his home, The Woodlands, near Bristol.

The Crescent was a native of Walsall and an early arrival on the scene in 1911. Two years later a move was made to Smethwick and production continued until 1915. The first models were rather crude aircooled 7/9 hp tandem seated machines with belt drive but by 1913 a neat well-built little friction drive side by side two seater was offered with five forward speeds, shaft-cum-chain final drive and 8 hp Precision or Blumfield engines. The example illustrated with its owner Frank Clarke in 1924 dates from 1914 and was recently unearthed intact in Haywards Heath.

William Cunningham's Midland Works at
Clitheroe, Lancs., were, until 1911, better known
for their Midland cycles and motorcycles,
although a light two seater with 7½ hp De Dion-
type engine had appeared briefly in 1905. The
LM (Little Midland) cyclecar was one of the first
British makes to appear, being first announced
in January 1911 and its specification altered
little. Initially offered with an aircooled J.A.P.
7 hp Vee twin engine set longitudinally in the
frame (watercooled from 1914) transmission
was by Renold chain via a two speed constant
mesh gearbox with dog clutches to a rear axle
with differential. Made later in Blackburn and
then Preston until 1922 it adhered to its cyclecar
image to the end.

By 1913 cyclecar rallies were popular events in
many parts of the country. In this scene from the
Cyclecar Club's Stratford-on-Avon rally can be
seen, left to right, a Leamington Spa-built
Invicta, a GN and a Morgan three wheeler. The
previous week the Invicta had run backwards
pinning its maker, Capt. H. E. Clarke, against a
wall, and cracking several ribs. In its account of
the journey of London members to Stratford, the
Cyclecar reported: "The evening at the Red Lion,
Banbury, was spent most merrily. Songs, a
breakdown competition, which Mr. Phillips was
the only one to solve, and several weird and
wonderful weight-lifting feats, saw the majority
into the wee sma' hours of the next day."

Of all the exponents of friction drive perhaps none was more enthusiastically promoted – or for so long – than the G.W.K.
Originally conceived by Arthur Grice, J. T. Wood and C. M. Keiller (of the marmalade firm) in a Beckenham stable, the car
started its production life at Home Works, Datchet, later moving to the infamous "Jam Factory" at Maidenhead. Captain
Wood always insisted that the G.W.K. was not a cyclecar, and insofar that it did not belong to the "belt drive and plywood
brigade" he was correct. With its rear-mounted, watercooled, Coventry-Simplex twin engine, and double disc friction drive
transmission it was, however, sufficiently unorthodox to be considered here. This example is seen outside Jesus Hospital,
Bray, in 1913.

This happy couple were only one satisfied family
out of 1069 to whom G.W.K. twins were sold up to
1915 and another hundred found homes in
1919/20. Although designed for marine work,
the engine performed well, propelling the little
car at about 35 mph and although advertised as
having "a gear for every gradient", the friction
drive was actually "fixed" so as to give four
forward speeds. Reverse was achieved by moving
the cork-faced driven disc along a shaft at right
angles to the flywheel (from which the drive was
taken) to a point beyond centre whence the action
would be reversed. The sharp-eyed reader will
observe that a section of the running board will
have to be removed when the side starting handle
is operated.

Despite its modest specification, the pre-war
G.W.K. was offered in two seater sports form – a
recipe which was more sporting than sports. A
1913 example is seen here, and in the
arrangement of the mechanical components it
echoes the touring model, whilst sporting a
"turtle back" tail and minus windscreen.

Alone of all the cyclecars, Morgan have survived into the eighties – albeit as a fully fledged Vee 8 engined sports car, but with some elements of suspension common to the very first cars to be shown in 1910. The son of a clergyman, H.F.S. Morgan designed and built the most popular, and undoubtedly the best, three wheeler in Britain, and his Malvern-based company manufactured no other type until 1936 – indeed, the three wheelers continued in production until July 1952. This line-up outside the Worcester Road works was taken circa 1913/14.

Despite the fact that it was a three wheeler, the Morgan was inherently stable, and therefore safe in operation, an attribute which endeared it to those of sporting persuasion. The combination of a lusty air-cooled (later watercooled) Vee twin J.A.P. or Precision engine, transmission by dog clutches and chains providing two speeds, and independent front suspension by sliding pillars and coil springs gave ample power, good road holding and excellent performance. W.G. McMinnies, seen here in "The Jabberwock" with passenger Frank Thomas, won the 1913 Amiens Grand Prix for Cyclecars (he was a staff member of The Cyclecar and Thomas was Hon. Sec. of the Cyclecar Club) at an average speed of 42 mph.

Flushed with success, the Morgan company announced a "G.P." Model for the 1914 season with overhead valve watercooled J.A.P. engine, and E.B. Ware is seen here testing his G.P. at Brooklands in 1915. In 1914, and driving a side valve Morgan, he had taken all Brooklands records in the 750 cc class, and at speed trials in July 1914 at the track he averaged 65 mph for the flying kilometre and 63 mph over the mile.

Designed by Captain John Carden, later Sir John (who also pleaded guilty to the A.V. Monocar and the Tamplin), the pre-Great War Carden was the archetype minimal cyclecar. Likened to an alligator with a sting in its tail, it was a single seater powered by a 4 hp single cylinder (later a Vee twin) aircooled J.A.P. which, initially, drove direct to the rear axle with no clutch or intermediate gearing. The driver thus had to push start the machine and leap in once the engine was firing! This crude arrangement was later modified to include a two speed countershaft gear and chain drive, in which form the car cost £55. The design was later taken up by Ward & Avey, makes of the A.V. monocar.

As we have seen, the first cyclecar boom of 1910-1925 witnessed the emergence of many firms offering kits of parts for cyclecar home builders, and doubtless many hundreds of D.I.Y. machines were constructed. El Pampéro, photographed here in 1914, is interesting in that not only is it an example of a fairly advanced and well-constructed amateur-designed machine, but miraculously it has survived unmodified to this day and is regularly fielded in VSCC events by Arthur Jeddere-Fisher. Otherwise known as the "Barron Ackroyd Special" after its original constructor who is believed to have been killed in the R.F.C. in W.W.1, it boasts a circa 1912 M.A.G. Vee twin air-cooled engine, and chain-cum-belt drive via a 3 speed and reverse Chater-Lee gearbox.

Designed by Ettore Bugatti and offered initially to Wanderer (who turned it down) the Bébé Peugeot was not, despite its appearances in the Cyclecar Grand Prix, a cyclecar at all. Over 3,000 were built by Peugeot before the war stopped production, however, and because its impact upon the pre-war cyclecar was comparable to that of the Austin Seven in 1922, it warrants mention. A true large car in miniature, it boasted an 856 cc watercooled four cylinder T head engine and an unusual transmission which relied upon twin concentric propeller shafts meshing with two rows of teeth on the crown wheel. Three speeds were provided in 1914, by which time the car cost £160. At the wheel of the lefthand car is the celebrated Peugeot driver Georges Boillot.

Electric vehicles were particularly popular in Germany, and the Berlin-built B.E.F. was current from 1907 until 1914 in both private and commercial form. A three wheeler, as illustrated in 1914 form, the B.E.F. employed an interesting front wheel drive designed by Victor Harborn who later founded the Geha concern which made similar vehicles. Elite took over Geha in 1917 and electric four wheelers made in Berlin were marketed under the Elite name.

Financed by the writer Sir Arthur Conan Doyle of Sherlock Holmes fame, the Tyseley works of A. W. Wall Ltd. produced a number of unorthodox designs alongside their Precision-engined Roc motorcycles. Licence-producers of the Briggs & Stratton (Smith) motorwheel, they also made this Wall Tricar (also known rudely as the "Roc egg") with sidecar type body and tiller steering. Available with 4/5 hp or 6 hp Precision engines, it was shaft driven and wheel steering was available from 1914. This example dates from 1912.

New Hudson were well-known bicycle and motorcycle makers, and like many of their competitors they built cyclecars from 1912 until 1924 at their Icknield Street works. Initially, this wire wheeled two seater was offered, powered by a 4½ hp single cylinder engine and with epicyclic gears. Post Great War versions were more sporting, however, with 8.96 hp Vee twin engines, three wheels only and chain drive.

Rudge-Whitworth were respected motorcycle producers and their Rudge cyclecar, announced in 1912, incorporated a number of the technical innovations of their Rudge-Multi motorcycle, including the variable gearing by belts and expanding pulley. Underslung at the front, and with staggered seating, it was of very low build – so much so that one luckless owner, returning late one night to Coventry, found himself pursued and laid hold of by several constables – who had failed to see him so low down and assumed that the vehicle was a runaway! With 750 cc single cylinder air-cooled engine, it lasted less than a year.

The Cockermouth-built Cumbria is notable for being the only known car made in Cumberland (now Cumbria). Built in an old tweed mill it was offered in monocar and two seater form with 6/8 hp and 8/10 hp J.A.P. engines and belt and chain drive respectively.

The Eric from Northampton was one of the earliest of the pre-first war cyclecars, being first offered in 1911. A three wheeler, it utilised a 6 hp watercooled flat twin engine, three speed gearbox and chain final drive to the single rear wheel. From 1913 a Salmons four cylinder engine was available, together with a closed coupé body.

Although closed bodies were unusual among cyclecars they were by no means unknown. The well-known Bowden Brake Co. of Tyseley were the manufacturers of the Tyseley, originally offered in three wheeled form in 1911, and their 1912 8 hp model announced at Olympia that year boasted an unusually pretty and refined coachbuilt coupé body. With Vee twin watercooled engine and two speed gearbox, it also enjoyed the luxury of shaft drive to a live rear axle. Offered in open form at 160 guineas, Tyseley's coupé was priced at 185 guineas.

Although early models of the Crescent were belt-driven, the combination of friction disc with this form of final drive was the exception rather than the rule. The 1914 Kennedy, built in Oakland Road, Clarendon Park, Leicester by Kennedy-Skipton & Co., was one of the few makes to combine the two, and unusually for so light a car it utilised a Salmon four cylinder engine of 1346 cc. The friction disc boasted a chrome leather facing, and the twin rear belts were of 9' rubber. 1914 was an inauspicious year in which to commence motor manufacture, however, and although the Kennedy struggled on until 1916, in its final form it employed a conventional three speed gearbox and overhead worm rear axle.

Chapter Three

Wind of Change and a Rearguard Action: The Twenties

The chronic civilian vehicle shortage which resulted from the four years' attrition of the Western Front initially gave the cyclecar a new lease of life, and the post-Armistice period saw a whole crop of newcomers and the re-emergence of many of the old names. Insurance companies still offered special policies for cyclecarists, *The Light Car and Cyclecar* continued its pre-war theme in advocating a really simple machine embodying all the principles laid down by the pioneers, and outwardly all was *bonhomie* as before.

Once the post-war demand had been catered for, however (and some of the newcomers were get-rich-quick profiteers whose products certainly did nothing to help the cyclecar image), it quickly became clear that all this post-war activity had effectively disguised the fact that the revolutionary spark – and much of the fun – had gone out of the "movement".

Whilst it was true that thousands of men (and women) had been trained in the driving, servicing and appreciation of the motor vehicle during the war years, and gratuities were often the exact amount required to purchase a cyclecar new, the war had left its mark on them in other ways. With broadened outlooks and a newly-acquired sophistication, they demanded something better than that which the old pre-war years had offered – and the gratuity went down as a deposit on a proper light car bought on hire purchase.

Redundant aircraft firms like A. V. Roe, Graham-White, Central Aircraft, and Kingsbury Aviation swelled the ranks of post-war constructors, but their contribution was short-lived, and with a gradual increase of interest in civil aviation the survivors thankfully sent the cyclecar packing. But it didn't happen overnight. Aero-engine makers Salmson of France purchased the French manufacturing rights to the G.N. and built several thousand in the first two years. They then developed from it their successful light sports car, and were followed by Amilcar, Senechal and others. A whole new breed of delightful French sports cars dominated the Twenties, and it was the cyclecar that had given them birth.

True, the first three years following the war witnessed the revival of the Cyclecar Grand Prix as an annual event, dozens of firms catered to the home builder offering engines, ready-made chassis and transmission systems, wheels and other essentials, and to some trench-weary soldiers the perky cyclecar must have provided an ideal opportunity to cock a snoot at the ruling classes and the establishment. Even Armstrong-Siddeley offered a cyclecar – the peculiar little cloverleaf Stoneleigh with air-cooled Vee-twin engine and central steering wheel – but they were careful not to call it an Armstrong-Siddeley.

But the wind of change was blowing. The motor industry slumped in 1920 and in 1921 *The Light Car and Cyclecar* asked the question "Are we too dignified?" and went on to say: "There was a time when we took keen delight in the unorthodox appearance of our machines, when we were not ashamed of the noise they made and when kerbside criticism left us unmoved – even pleased – and when, in the joy of a new discovery, we cared naught what the world said and went rejoicing on our way. Alas! Such times were too good to last; it was not expected that the early ultra-simple cyclecar could resist the overwhelming force urging it onwards to perfection, and, obeying the irresistible impulse, the cyclecar as we enthusiasts knew it in 1912, has with few exceptions ceased to exist."

In Britain, certainly, this was true. Contraptions like the Gibbons and the surprisingly practical little Harper Runabout continued to cater for a few die-hards, and the sporting Morgan was well-entrenched, but in fact there were few who would have echoed "The Call of the Cyclecar", a poem written by a reader and published in *The Light Car and Cyclecar* on 1st April 1922:
"The road is calling, calling,
    and I only want to feel
The breezes rushing by me,
    as I sit behind the wheel.
My car is old, and out of date,
    and yet, what do I care!
I can't afford a new one,
    and Spring is in the air!
Ah, ye befurred vulgarians!
    Ye bloated profiteers!
Who loll in corded cushions,
    while a hired chauffeur steers!
You loudly talk of motoring,
    yet know not what it means,
For the joy of life is absent
    from your lordly limousines!
You patronize us humble folk,
    yet I would rather, far,
Plug noisily through England
    on my ancient cyclecar.

WIND OF CHANGE AND A REARGUARD ACTION: THE TWENTIES

In Germany, and to a degree, France, it was a different story. Both had suffered economically from the war, but Germany's problems were exacerbated by the reparations demands of the League of Nations, and France's by the fact that much of the conflict had been fought on her soil. The cyclecar was destined to have a longer life in these countries than elsewhere.

Spain supported a small cyclecar industry which had grown from the Barcelona sport of "Down Cars" – a species of engine-less soap-box racers – but was hampered by the inherent poverty of the population and the unsuitability of light and flimsy construction for use on her appalling roads.

In America, Ford's Model T and its main rival Chevrolet effectively killed the post-war cyclecar in much the same way as they eventually decimated that country's motorcycle industry, and in Britain Rover's air-cooled Eight and the unorthodox little oil-cooled Belsize-Bradshaw pioneered really cheap light cars of more substantial construction. The arrival of the Austin Seven in 1922 was, however, the most significant post-War event in the killing off of the cyclecar. Like the Bébé Peugeot of a decade earlier, it was a "real" car in miniature, and sold like hot cakes, eventually prompting other large manufacturers – notably Triumph – to offer a similar light car. Jowett, of course, had been quietly making their agricultural little twins up in Yorkshire for some years, and these too became popular.

Even the Cyclecar Club changed its name. In 1919 it became the Junior Car Club since, as Armstrong bluntly pointed out, the "cycle-car" had become to many a dirty word, and in any event no longer represented the backbone of the club.

It is significant that even in 1914 S. F. Edge declined (albeit courteously) the Presidency of The Cyclecar Club – his subsequent involvement with A.C. light cars would have sorted ill with such an appointment, but the fact is lightcarists generally looked down on cyclecars, and this snobbish attitude had gathered some momentum by 1919; even in 1915 a change to the Junior Automobile Club had been mooted, unsuccessfully. In the latter year, however, the growth of the light car faction within the Club hastened the raising of the eligibility limit from 1,100 to 1,500cc, with affiliation with the R.A.C. (and increased fees) instead of the A.-C.U.

In the event, and following the formation of the Junior Car Club, it was decided that four wheeled members should affiliate to the R.A.C. and three wheelers to the A.-C.U., with the following revised definitions of vehicles eligible for J.C.C. activities:

Light cars up to 1500cc with four seats weighing at least 15cwt, or up to 1100cc with two seats weighing 13cwt.

Cyclecars up to 1100cc with a catalogue weight for an open two seater of 9cwt.

The decision in 1925 to exclude three wheelers (and thus, Morgans) from their prestigious 200 Mile Race at Brooklands underlined the distance which the J.C.C. had travelled since the formation of the Cyclecar Club in 1912, and by this time it had in any event become more and more a racing club and social events, rallies and picnics were less and less a feature of club activities. The cyclecar had grown up.

The tiny 348 cc Skeoch was a latecomer to the cyclecar world, being first announced in 1921. Powered by a single cylinder Precision engine driving through a Burman two speed gearbox to chain final drive, it was built at the Burnside Motor Works, Dalbeattie, and is notable for having been probably the only true cyclecar built in Scotland. It was designed by J. B. Skeoch (an ex-employee of Belhaven Engineering & Motor Co. of Wishaw, the builders of the Belhaven lorry), but the works burned down after only ten examples had been built.

The original concept of the ultra-simple cyclecar was waning rapidly in popularity by 1921. Notwithstanding this a number of uncompromisingly spartan vehicles continued to appear, and of these the Chadwell Heath-built Gibbons was typical. Like the Cricket, L.A.D. and post-second war Gordon, it carried its engine in an exposed position on the offside amidships – in this case a 688 cc Coventry-Victor flat twin, although 349 cc Precision and 488 cc Blackburne singles were also available. Two speeds were provided – by high ratio belt to the nearside rear wheel, low to the offside, and bodies were of plywood. With a six year production span it must have had some merit!

Even a design as uncompromisingly spartan as the Gibbons was forced, eventually, to make some concessions, and the example illustrated offered not only chain drive in place of belts, but four seats with an Auster screen for the rear seat passengers, a hood, more substantial front wings and a partially cowled Vee twin Blackburne engine. The very basic centre pivot steering with control by cable and bobbin was retained, however, as was the plywood bodywork, pram rear springs and central helical front spring. Road tax, registration fee and number plates were included, however.

A good impression of the driver's view of the road from the pilot's seat of a Carden monocar may be gained from this photograph taken in April 1919. Note the large bore exhaust pipe, which probably necessitated a slow run past the horse and doubtless accounts for the carrier's stoney stare. One rear lamp and no reflectors were sufficient to comply with the lighting regulations of the day.

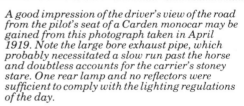

Captain (later Sir) John Carden, was an incurable experimenter and inventor, concerning himself with everything from ultra-light aircraft and amphibious tanks to cyclecars. Having sold his pre-war design to A.V., he then sold his post-war design to E. A. Tamplin. In 1920, he was back however with a rear engined model powered by two stroke flat-twin engine of 707 cc in-unit with the axle and driving direct through reduction gears to produce two speeds, and he is here pictured in this model. His untimely death in an air crash in 1935 stemmed the flow of ideas, but as the New Carden the car remained available until 1925, from new premises in Willesden.

E. A. Tamplin was the the proprietor of the
Railway Garage, Kingston Road, Staines, and
was, prior to 1st November 1919, the sole
distributors of the Ascot-built Carden monocar,
having contracted for the whole of the firm's
output that year. In the November he purchased
all manufacturing rights to the then-existing
Carden design, and thereafter the car was known
as the Tamplin. The Tamplin featured a large
8 hp aircooled J.A.P. Vee twin set frontally and
longitudinally in the frame, driving by primary
chain through a three speed Sturmey-Archer
gearbox by long single belt to the nearside rear
wheel. Offered as two seater or monocar at £150
and 120 guineas respectively it adopted all chain
drive in 1922 and was available, latterly in
Cheam, until 1927. Some 2,000 were built.

With a chassis weight of only 6½ cwt, high geared (though light) steering, and excellent roadholding allied to an excellent power to weight ratio, G.N.'s were popular entrants in rallies and sporting events, and unlike many of their contemporaries they were not only fast but reliable. R.C. "Rex" Mundy amply demonstrated the latter attribute under R.A.C. observation in 1920 when he drove his G.N. — seen here at the start — from London to Edinburgh without stopping the engine (even during meals!). Note the combination of electric (head) and acetylene (side) lights. Post-war cars were constructed with steel rather than ash frames at the old British Gregoire works at Wandsworth, conventional steering boxes replaced wire and bobbin and chain final drive was standardised. Fifty cars a week were being turned out in 1920/21, and what had been one of the first became the most popular British cyclecar.

Such was the light build of the average cyclecar, giving an excellent power to weight ratio, that performance often belied frail appearances. The whole cult of the cyclecar revolved around rallies, races, and the romance of the open road during the boom years 1910-1925 and the sporting capabilities of many makes were enthusiastically displayed by their sponsors. Here Captain Archie Frazer-Nash (the "N" of GN) puts his G.N. Special "Kim" into a controlled drift round the first bend of the Shelsey Walsh hill climb during the Midland Automobile Club's event on 29th July 1922. He finished the climb, after crashing, with both offside wheels buckled and one tyre off!

In March 1919, The Cyclecar Club changed its name to the Junior Car Club. The cyclecar was dying, if not dead, and it was a sign of the times. In March 1921 the J.C.C. took the important step of booking Brooklands for a 200 Miles Race in the October (it continued annually until 1928 at the track), the first big International race to be held there. Here Archie Frazer-Nash and his travelling mechanic L. A. Cushman change a piston in 42 minutes in the 1922 200 Mile Race in which they competed in the 1100 cc class.

The light handling of the average cyclecar had made it popular with women drivers from the very beginning, and particularly so following the emancipation women had enjoyed during the Great War. G.W.K. aimed their post-war advertising programme directly at the distaff side with their "Miss G.W.K." and here G.N. demonstrate the post-war model's ease of handling and starting. Note the rear mounted kick starter and centre "Cyclops" headlamp – now powered by electricity.

We could not resist including this G.N. complete with "the men with the sheet", a recurring feature of early motorcar photography. The idea was that the sheet would blot out the distracting (and frequently sordid) background, and thus concentrate the reader's full attention on the lines and detail of the car. Normally the sheet was of such blazing whiteness that some of the detail was obliterated by the glare, but there is no danger of such an occurrence here!

The similarity between the pre-war Carden monocar and the post-war A.V. is highlighted here, as also is the problem of courting in a single seater! The road surface is typical of many to have been found in rural England during the twenties, and the two gallon petrol can on the running board is a reminder that petrol filling stations were few and far between in 1920/21 and petrol pumps with bulk storage even rarer.

Just how rural British country roads were during the twenties may be gathered from this illustration of an A.V. two seater taken at Crocknorth Corner in Surrey. By this time the A.V. had acquired a redesigned Vee-fronted dummy radiator, electric lighting and side by side seating, but the engine – usually an 1100 cc aircooled Vee twin by J.A.P. or Blackburne – still resided in the tail.

As might be expected, the combination of a large twin cylinder motorcycle-type engine and a light simple integral body and chassis presented endless opportunities for the enthusiast wishing sheer performance at the expense of comfort and many cyclecars were made to "go" indecently fast. Just such an exponent was Major R.C. Empson whose aptly named and somewhat "tweeked" A.V. monocar "Icanopit" was a regular contender at Brooklands where this photograph was taken. Late in 1920 Empson took the two hour record in the Light Car Class at 59.3 mph, only to lose it shortly afterwards to Cocker's rear engined Crouch.

Although, strictly speaking, the post-Great War Warren-Lambert was no longer a cyclecar, it is included here as an illustration of the fate which befell many of the simpler successful pre-war types following the Armistice. In fact, 1914 models built at Shepherd's Bush had employed four cylinder watercooled engines and postwar production from new premises in Richmond standardised the four cylinder 1330 cc Alpha unit. A super sports good for 60 mph employed the 1½ litre Coventry Simplex allied to an enormous burnished copper exhaust exposed at the side of the car. These models had outgrown the market for which the Warren-Lambert had been designed, however, and production ceased in 1922.

Although the cyclecar achieved a peak of popularity in Britain, France, Germany and America, examples were made in virtually every country in the world, including India. The Bjering hailed from Norway, where it was particularly useful on narrow country roads which had not been fully cleared of snow. Initially fitted with an aircooled Vee four engine amidships and tandem seated, the Bjering steered from the rear and was used by country police. Arrested wrongdoers sat in the front seat where the policeman could keep tabs on them! Later models employed metal, as opposed to the earlier wooden, bodies and a rear mounted four cylinder engine. Skis in place of front wheels were an available option.

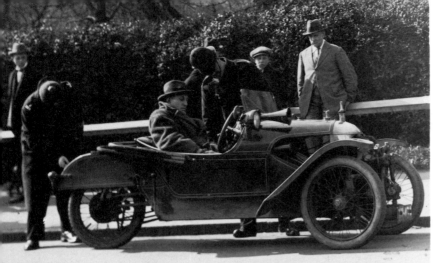

One tends to associate police persecution of motorists with the very early days following the so-called Emancipation Act of 1896 and particularly in the early Edwardian period. The fact is that the police disliked cyclecars as a breed and there is evidence to suggest that the noisier and faster makes attracted a good deal more police attention after 1910 than their larger brothers. This luckless Morgan owner is receiving attention from two members of "the law", and warnings of police traps were a frequent feature of The Cyclecar before and after the Great War.

Although there was much talk of mass production in the cyclecar world in the immediate post-war and car starved period, few makes actually achieved it and photographic views like this one of the Morgan works in Pickersleigh Road in 1920 can be misleading. In fact there are about 27 cars illustrated, which was a respectable production from so small a factory.

Following the formation of the Junior Car Club from the old Cyclecar Club, the four wheeled members affiliated themselves to the R.A.C. and the three wheelers became affiliated to the Autocycle Union – the governing body for motorcyclists. It is only natural, therefore, to see this 1922 Morgan in the showroom of the Homax Garage – predominantly a motorcycle dealer's.

But eventually this split between three and four wheelers was destined to have repercussions which, had they been foreseen, would probably have prevented the decision being taken. Following a disastrous accident to Edward Bradford Ware (who was the Morgan expert, chief of the J.A.P. experimental department and an old member of the Cyclecar Club), in the 1924 200 Mile Race – he is seen here in the pits before the accident – three wheelers were banned from the event. Morgans protested n vain, but Ware suffered shocking injuries from which he took three years to recover, and that was that.

Despite its sporting potential, however, the family appeal of the Morgan was not overlooked and as early as 1912 a four seater prototype was built. A Dorman engined four wheeler was not, however, proceeded with but production family models were offered from 1915. The standard two seater was also equally at home on mundane duties. This 1919 example was operated by Mr. Brackensey, a representative for the Graham-White Aviation Co. of Hendon who, doubtless, was later issued with a car of their own manufacture with which to carry out his travelling duties.

It is not generally known, but the Co-operative Wholesale Society built not only lorries and cars (under the C.W.S. Bell name), but at its cycle works at Tyseley in Birmingham from 1922, the C.W.S. cyclecar. Totally in keeping with the Co-op's cloth cap image of working class thrift, and utilising a watercooled version of the 8 hp J.A.P. Vee twin engine employed in their Federation motorcycle, the little C.W.S. drove by chain through a three speed gear box, but at £150 and with only three wheels it was no competition for Austin's Seven.

The Royal Ruby was once a leading make of motorcycle on the British market, hailing originally from Ancoats, Manchester, and finally from Bradshaw Gate, Bolton. Two attempts to break into the ultra-light car market: the first between 1913/14 was a pure cyclecar with the inevitable J.A.P. Vee twin 10 hp engine, two speeds and a choice of shaft and belt drive, but in 1927 the company tried again. This latter attempt came late, and is illustrated here. A light three wheeler with a choice of 350 cc Villiers or 500 cc single cylinder J.A.P. and a tortuous system of chains driving the rear wheel, it lasted but one season.

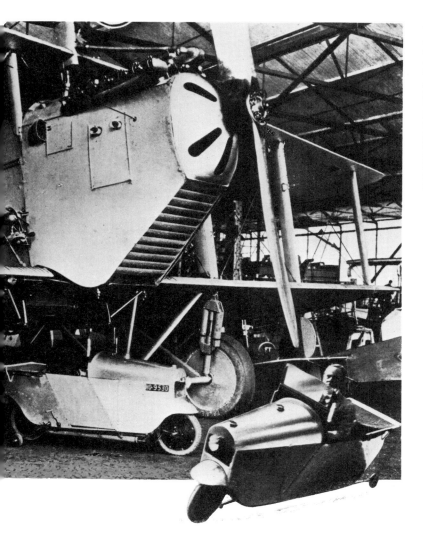

To counteract the doldrums which faced the aviation industry following the Armistice and before the growth of civil aviation later in the twenties, many aircraft manufacturers tried their hand at car, motorcycle and scooter production in a desperate effort to keep their factories going, and A. V. Roe was no exception. Crossley had taken a controlling interest in the firm in 1920 and various experimental light cars were built under the Avro name. This monocar, powered by a 2½ hp Barr & Stroud front mounted two stroke engine driving by chains from a three speed gearbox, appeared in 1923. It boasted channel steel chassis members and quarter elliptic springing back and front. At £75 it offered 25 mph and 100 mpg.

The Chertsey-built Xtra was little more than a motorised sidecar and it is appropriate, therefore, that it should have made its debut at the December 1921 Motor Cycle show. Powered by a 2¾ hp Villiers engine (269 cc) driving through a two speed chain drive the design incorporated a friction drive on to the rear wheel pulley. At £95 one suffered acetylene lamps as well, and the Xtra faded away in 1924.

*The Hanomag took its name from its sponsors, the **Han**noversche **Ma**schinenbau A.G. vorm Georg Eggestorff. Until 1924 they were better known for locomotives and steamlorries but in that year they introduced their 2/10PS two seater, which promptly earned itself the nickname of the Kommisbrot (army loaf) because of its shape in coupé form. Despite a specification which included rear mounted single o.h.v. 499 cc engine, narrow track, no differential and chain final drive, nearly 16,000 found buyers up to 1928.*

Although designed by René Tondeur, The R.T.C. was British and built in Croydon. Its transmission was interesting in that the aircooled Vee twin Blackburn 8 hp engine drove twin belts direct to the rear axle, a centrifugal governor automatically varying the effective diameter of the belt pulleys to give a variable gear. The chassis was made of wood, and the front spring resembled that found on a perambulator.

Although Louis Blériot's Blériot Aéronautique at Suresnes built a twin cylinder two stroke engined shaft driven cyclecar from 1921 until 1922, it appears to have had no connection or similarity with the Addlestone-built Blériot Whippet. Made by the Air Navigation & Engineering Company (and designed by George Herbert Jones of Shrewsbury), who also built the J.A.P. engined Eric Longden light cars, the Whippet employed an unusual infinitely variable drive by belt and pulley, similar to that found on the Zenith Gradua motorcycle, the engine being a centrally mounted aircooled Vee twin Blackburne. During its relative long life between 1920 and 1927, the car acquired first chain drive and reverse and latterly a conventional gearbox and shaft drive.

The controversy which revolved around the necessity or otherwise of a proper differential spawned a number of interesting designs during the 1920's and the Bolton-built M.B. (or Merrall-Brown) was one of these. Like the first Ashton-Evans and some models of the post second war Isetta, it was a four wheeler but placed the rear wheels a mere eight inches or so apart, giving the appearance of a three wheeler. This model is illustrated, but whilst initially offered with watercooled Vee twin Precision engine, two speeds, acetylene lighting and chain drive, it had by 1920 become a conventional four wheeler with four cylinder Coventry Simplex engine

The C.F.B. shown here in its native Upper Norwood is interesting since its designer and sponsor C. F. Beauvais was also responsible later for the "waterfall" grill motif on the Kaye Don Singers in 1931/32, then designed the Avon Standards, improved the looks of the Coventry-Victor three wheeler, revamped the bodywork of the Crossley three litre and turned the Lanchester Ten into a concours winner. His own C.F.B. was, however less successful. Announced in 1920, its 8 hp Vee twin engine drove by shaft to a cone, thence to a fibre faced disc which drove another shaft and bevels to a countershaft on which were mounted twin pulleys from which ran rubber belts to the rear wheels. This Pandora's box apparently produced an infinitely variable gearing.

Advertised by its makers as "the smallest cyclecar in the world", the Custer (mis-reported in the popular press as the "Cootie") is something of a mystery. The absence of cooling ducts or a radiator would seem to point to electric power, and the fact that Lupino Lane (seen here arriving at the London Hippodrome) used the car on stage in his act, adds weight to this theory. The number plate is of regulation size and the electric lights are real enough, so pedal power is ruled out.

Billed in 1921 as the cheapest three speed car on the market, the diminutive Metro-Tyler was built by a company formed from the post-war fusion of motorcycle builders Metro Mfg. & Engineering Co., of Saltley, and the Tyler Apparatus Co., of Bannister Road, Kilburn Lane. Offered with hood, windscreen and electric lighting set at £149, it was powered by a 5/6 hp aircooled twin cylinder two stroke unit made up of two Metro motorcycle engines. Three speeds were provided with belt final drive, although chain options were offered in 1923. A utility model sold for only £125. The lower picture was taken during the 1922 London-Edinburgh Trial, and shows a Metro-Tyler ahead of a Talbot 8/18 light car.

Thompson Bros of Bilston, Staffs., were well known boiler makers who entered the three wheeled cyclecar market in 1919 with the well made and quite successful T.B. It was built in their redundant aircraft department and initially offered with J.A.P. or Precision Vee twin aircooled engines, a two speed gearbox and the refinement of shaft drive to the single rear wheel. By 1921 a watercooled Blackburne had been standardised which, although difficult to start, gave a quieter and more spirited performance. Initially priced at £200 and later £250, the T.B. was redesigned with a 1084 cc British Anzani engine in 1924, in which year production ceased in favour of small three wheeled petrol tankers for airfield use.

The Simplic started life in Cobham in 1914 as a simple belt driven machine costing only £75. Unlike many of its fellows, however, it survived the war period and emerged in redesigned form in 1923 with chain transmission as illustrated here, although the large J.A.P. power unit remained unchanged. Post-war production, such as it was (probably only two cars!), centred on Weybridge, where even the proximity of Brooklands track could not sustain it. Its sponsors had previously been responsible for the three wheeled Autotrix in the same town.

The *Iliffe*-produced Light Car *at one stage propounded that no one should buy a cyclecar until all makers had standardised their layouts, transmissions and general design. This suggestion brought hoots of derision from Temple Press's Light Car & Cyclecar and, indeed, it is one of the fascinations of the cyclecar that manufacturers were free to adopt virtually whatever system they pleased, and did! The Anglo-French Trident was to have been made by Vickers Ltd., and could not have been more unorthodox. Suspension relied upon an interlinked arrangement of cantilever springs, seating was in tandem and the driven single front wheel supported on one side the watercooled vertical twin engine and on the other, the three speed gearbox, clutch and magneto! It was priced at £160.*

Better known for their motorcycles, Baughan also built cyclecars sporadically between 1920 and 1929, initially from premises in Harrow and, from 1921 in Stroud, Gloucestershire. At least one has survived, and follows the well-trodden pattern of many of its competitors with a large aircooled Vee twin front mounted engine (J.A.P. or Blackburne were offered), Sturmey-Archer motorcycle gearbox and chain final drive.

Apart from the Morgan, the three wheeler was never over-popular in Britain and Coventry-Premier were one of the better known makers of the early twenties. Built in Coventry by a well known bicycle and motorcycle manufacturer and designed by G.W.A. Brown, it initially employed a watercooled Vee twin of their own make and enclosed chain final drive. Prophetically it was announced at the same time as the Kidderminster-built Castle Three who advocated a four cylinder engine and shaft drive and quickly followed suit after acquisition by Singer in 1920. In final form it was a cheap version of the Singer Ten with four wheels.

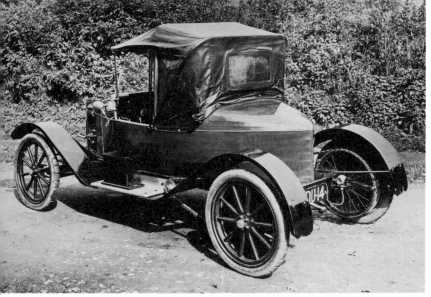

Although the Coventry-Victor company did not produce a car until 1926 (and then, a three wheeler) their Mr. Weaver designed an interesting four wheeler in 1919 which is illustrated here. Employing the Coventry-Victor 8 hp aircooled flat twin engine and shaft and bevel drive, chain, and twin Whittle belt final drive (a complicated system) with a Sturmey-Archer three speed gearbox, the car was attractive. The body, designed by Mr. Budge of Standard, consisted of ash battens covered with doped, painted and varnished canvas on an ash frame. Mr. Weaver's syndicate hoped to sell it for £150.

The Economic was the archetype "flying bedroom slipper" type of cyclecar which, in simplicity and crudity of construction, was seldom surpassed. Little more than an unsprung ash buckboard (similar to the American Briggs & Stratton Flyer), it was steered by the single front wheel, accommodated two in wickerwork bucket seats and was powered by a flat twin two stroke – probably a Johnson – of under 200 cc. Weighing only 150 lb and driving via friction disc by chain to the offside rear wheel, its maximum speed was 30 mph and the price – £60! It was offered only in 1921 and 1922.

Designed by Dudley Taylor and built in 1920 at 452 Moseley Road, Birmingham, the Gerald was another cyclecar which dispensed with a differential by placing the rear wheels close together – in this case two feet apart. Although the watercooled 8 hp J.A.P. engine was orthodox enough, the drive was transmitted by a system of chain and belt embodying an ingenious variable gearing which maintained the belt at normal tension no matter what ratio was employed. No reverse gear was provided, and the independent Ferodo cone clutch could be "locked out" on a ratchet to facilitate moving the car by hand. The car has an exceptionally long wheelbase for a two seater.

Following the Great War and exacerbated by the reparation demands of the League of Nations, Germany's economic situation deteriorated until the collapse of the Mark in 1922. In such a climate, and indeed throughout the twenties and thirties, unorthodox minimal machines found a ready market and the cyclecar survived far longer than elsewhere. The tiny S.B. (Slaby Beringer) was designed by Dr. Slaby and built in Berlin, and comprised a single seater chassisless wooden body powered by an electric motor and tiller steered. D.K.W. took over the design and later models had D.K.W. motor cycle engines but Gamages sold the electric version in 1920 in London for £150

Despite an enthusiastic write-up in the contempoary Motor Sport – possibly influenced by an advertisement taken in the same issue! – the odd little Gnome (later Nomad) arrived far too late in Britain for its crude specification to gain acceptance. Made only from 1925 to 1926 in South West London, it eschewed springs altogether, relying upon balloon tyres at 6 lb per square inch, and the steel and plywood body acted as chassis as well. Add to this a Villiers 343 cc two stroke engine, friction disc transmission and single chain drive and the recipe for failure was complete.

Bearing in mind its unsophisticated specification, the Hamilton, built by D. J. Smith & Co., of Wickford in Essex, between 1921 and 1925, enjoyed a longer life than most of the post Great War cyclecars. Unusual features were the dummy oval radiator and steering arm above the front axle, but the mechanics – 9 hp Precision Vee twin, and friction drive through chains – were undistinguished. From £230 in 1921 the makers dropped the price in 1925 (in desperation, possibly) to £150 but the Austin Seven was by then well established. This car carries another example of an early trade plate.

L. A. Durant's unconventional L.A.D. cyclecar enjoyed a relatively long production life from 1913 until 1926, although several types were offered during this period. Originally a Carden-type monocar with rear-mounted Stag engine, post-war versions like this 1923 example were little more than motorised sidecars with tiller steering and a choice of 350 cc Broler single engine or 700 cc twin. By 1934, Mr. Durant was offering kits to convert motorcycle combinations into three-wheeled vans like the early Reliant.

Despite its somewhat ugly and rather outdated appearance, Lambert Engineering's Harrow-built Lecoy nevertheless enjoyed some success, winning a Gold Medal in the London-Exeter Trial of 1922, a year after being introduced. Despite this, however, and the economy of an 8 hp aircooled J.A.P. engine, friction drive coupled to a price of £185 attracted few and the Lecoy was gone by 1923.

Built at St. Etienne, Loire, the Monotrace was one of that select band of cyclecars which relied upon only two road wheels, augmented by two small "outriggers" to support it when standing still. Based on the German Mauser Einspurato, and steered by large handlebars with the two seats in tandem, the Monotrace employed a 510 cc single cylinder watercooled engine, a motorcycle gearbox and chain final drive. It enjoyed a relatively long production run from 1924 until 1930. This is a 1927 example.

Although few cyclecars were built in Britain after 1925, the majority of those which enjoyed limited success fell into the three wheeled category. Omega had been well known for their motorcycles in Wolverhampton and Coventry since 1909 and the little Omega Eight appeared only two years before the company's demise in 1927. This quite attractive little machine cost only £90 and followed the well worn formula of a 980 cc J.A.P. driving the single rear wheel by chain. It was billed as "the three wheeler that runs like a four".

One of the most prolific designers of small cars, Marcel Violet had a hand in not only the Violet-Bogey, Alcyon, Major, Deguingand, Mourre, Sicam, and post second-war Bernardet but also the relatively successful Sima-Violet built at Courbevoie on the Seine from 1924 until 1929. All of these makes except Violet-Bogey employed two stroke engines, in which Violet specialised, and the late-arriving and unconventional Sima-Violet was no exception. A horizontally opposed aircooled transversely front mounted engine of only 496 cc drove through a two speed gearbox mounted on the rear axle. With similar transverse front springing, the Alcyon was virtually identical.

The only Italian cyclecar to attain international currency, the Temperino was intentionally mass produced with universal appeal, and its design was established even before the Great War. As cyclecars go, it was well made and relatively sophisticated with a radiator reminiscent of the Fiat 501. Here, J. S. Wood is seen in London with a 1921 model, which, unusually (and like the Edwardian Robinson) cooled its Vee twin engine with its own exhaust gases.

It has been said of Arthur Grice (at the wheel of a 1921 Unit) that he was "congenitally incapable of pursuing an idea beyond the prototype stage" (Lord Montagu: "Lost Causes of Motoring") and the evidence seems to support such a theory. Having ruined G.W.K. by endeavouring to provide post-war models with a more acceptable front-engined four cylinder model, he departed in 1920 to rescusitate Rotary Units Ltd., at Wooburn, a company he had formed eight years earlier to develop a pumping engine with "five eccentric cylinders" – predictably a failure. Here he made the Unit – initially a return to first principles with a twin cylinder 998 cc Bovier engine mounted at the rear and friction drive, but later bowing to public opinion with front mounted two and four cylinder engines as illustrated here. By 1923 Unit were out of business and Grice was back at G.W.K., where in 1927 he made a three wheeler with rear-mounted V-twin J.A.P. engine. A price of £90 was fixed, but it never went into production.

The Manchester-built Seal was similar to the last models of the L.A.D. and it shared a comparable life-span from 1912 until 1924. Resembling a motorcycle and sidecar combination, it was nevertheless controlled from within the "sidecar" where both driver and passenger sat side by side, and employed wheel steering. Power was provided by a 770 cc (later 980 cc) J.A.P. aircooled Vee twin mounted in the same position as that of a motorcycle, and the drive transmitted through a three speed Sturmey-Archer hub (later Burman) gearbox with chain final drive. Shaft drive was tried in 1920. A full four seater "Family" model appeared in the early twenties.

There can have been few designers more iconoclastic than Alfred Angas Scott, whose inimitable water cooled two stroke motorcycle lives on today in the Silk machines. His little three wheeled Sociable started life during the Great War as a prototype combination machine gun carrier, and employed the same vertical two stroke engine as the motorcycles. Going one better than the Seal, however, the bodywork enveloped the engine which drove by shaft to the offside rear wheel.

Italy has produced many advanced and innovative automobiles over the years, and although shortlived, the San Giusto cyclecar built in Milan and Trieste was no exception. Employing independent suspension on all wheels by transverse leaf springs and a narrow backbone-type chassis, it boasted front wheel brakes in 1924 (in which year they were first adopted by Rolls-Royce!), four forward speeds and a rear mounted aircooled 748 cc four cylinder engine. This 1923 chassis is in the Museo dell'Automobile in Turin.

Like the air-cooled Rover Eight, the oil-cooled Belsize-Bradshaw designed by Granville Bradshaw for the old established Manchester Belsize concern may be considered a "half-way house" in the evolution of the post Great War light car from the cyclecar. Introduced in 1921, it was made in respectable numbers until 1924 in both side valve and overhead valve form and enthusiastically espoused by agents like Gordon Watney. Despite an in-unit three speed gearbox, shaft and bevel drive and a much quieter performance than its aircooled rivals, it acquired the nickname of the "old boiler" and speeded its makers into bankruptcy.

Just as the 1912 Bébé Peugeot had set the trend away from cyclecars of the simpler type in motion, so the Austin Seven introduced in 1922 ensured their rapid demise – in Britain at least. Although originally hailed by the press as a cyclecar, the Seven was truly a large car in miniature, its watercooled four cylinder engine, three speed gearbox, shaft drive and full differential live axle showing up its lesser competitors unfavourably. As demand increased, the mass production facilities of the giant Longbridge works enabled the price to be progressively reduced until, in 1934, a £100 model was produced. Few could compete with that.

Founded by Ebenezer Richardson, who produced household gadgets and toys in his garden shed in Holmehirst Road, Sheffield, C. E. Richardson & Co. Ltd. commenced production of cyclecars in 1919 at Finbat Works, Napier Street, where Finbat toys were also made. With the usual large J.A.P. or Precision Vee twin engine providing the power, drive was by friction discs to a single chain final drive. Painted in the same kiln in which the toys had previously been finished the £200 Richardson was also offered as a light van and its ugly appearance was later improved by a vertical dummy radiator.

Designed by Senor J. M. Armangue, a pioneer cyclecarist and "down car" enthusiast in Spain who was killed in a flying accident in October 1917, the David owed its origins to its sponsor's love of bob sleighing. Finding no snow on arrival at an important contest, he devised a wheeled bob sleigh and "down car" racing (which we would call a soap box Derby) was born. The first engine fitted to a "down car" by Jose Maria Armangue was intended merely to propel it to the nearest hill top from which it could coast down again by gravity. From this evolved the David, best known of all Spanish designs and fitted usually with four cylinder o.h.v. or side valve engines by M.A.G., Hispano-Suiza or Ballot with belt and variable pulley transmission.

The start of a cyclecar event at Barcelona in 1917. In the foreground is a Diaz y Grillo, powered by a two cylinder two stroke Blumfield engine. Behind it is a David, and numerous motorcycle combinations are also preparing for the fray.

Designed by Mauve, who later built the more conventional Mauve car under his own name, the Elfe was built at Vierzon and was first shown as a front engined belt driven monocar at the 1919 Paris Salon. The 1920 competition version (which took part unsuccessfully in the Le Mans Cyclecar Grand Prix from 1920 until 1922) drove by chain from a rear mounted Vee twin aircooled 1100 cc Anzani, the passenger sitting immediately behind the driver with his legs on either side of him braced on footrests outside the car! An Elfe won its class in the flying kilometre at the Nice Trials in 1921.

It would be difficult to find a more ugly and unprepossessing cyclecar than the poor little Huddersfield and Mirfield-built L.S.D. Like the Castle Three, it advocated three Sankey artillery wheels, an unhappy combination. The good old J.A.P. Vee twin was again used, allied to a three speed transmission by shaft and final chain and surprisingly some 640 found buyers – latterly with M.A.G. and Blackburne engines. The company was bought by Ivor Blakey in 1924 and following his death the remains of 26 L.S.D.s were found and await restoration!

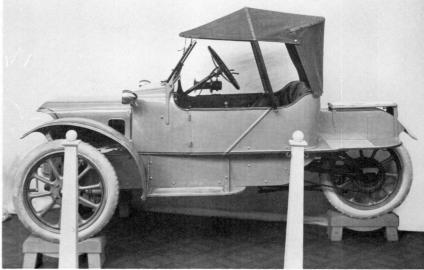

To a greater or lesser degree principles learned in aircraft construction during the Great War were to find application in the motor industry from the Hispano-Suiza H 6 B down to the humbler Avro monocar. A number of constructors, including the sponsors of the French Traction Aérienne from Neuilly, Seine, the Eolia and the Hélica, attempted to take matters a stage further. Such a man was Marcel Leyat whose Leyat endeavoured to adapt not only an aircraft type fuselage to a road going vehicle, but also propulsion by air-screw. Various experiments were carried out from 1913 until circa 1927 with flat twin A.B.C. and three cylinder Anzani engines. This example has survived.

In 1920 Bourbeau and Devaux sold out their interests in the Bédélia to their Paris agents M. Binet who, between 1920 and 1925, contracted out the manufacture to L. Mahieux et Cie of Levallois-Perret. Although the postwar models resisted the temptation to become conventional light cars, they put on weight, eventually acquired side by side seating and never recaptured their pre-war popularity. This 1921 example with "Cyclops" centre headlight still adhered to belt drive and a large Vee twin aircooled engine, but introduced a crude exposed three speed gear by means of friction discs on a sliding shaft. Depression of the clutch pedal fully also operated the brake.

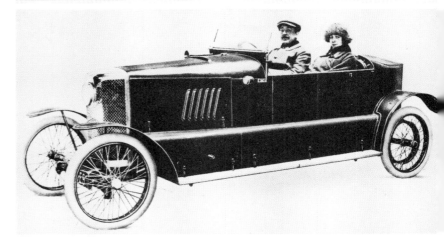

The Jappic made in 1925 by Jarvis & Sons of Wimbledon, the well known coachbuilders, was the only cyclecar designed specifically for record breaking. A chain driven monocar suspended on quarter elliptics front and rear, it offered a choice of 350 cc or 500 cc J.A.P. motorcycle engines suitable for class I or J record attempts in the days when such activities could be quite profitable. For the sportsman who wished to try his hand at the under-500 cc records, the Jappic was ideal, had an astonishing performance and actually took several World's Records.

Made by a firm who specialised in plywood cyclecar kits for home builders, the Bow-V-Car, like many of its contemporaries, made Upper Norwood its stamping ground. Employing integral construction of body and chassis it was late on the scene in 1922 and lasted only a year. Its aircooled 10 hp Precision engine was totally enclosed and relied upon a special rotary suction fan, the Jardine four speed gearbox incorporated both clutch and cockpit-operated kick starter and final drive was by chain. There were few takers.

With its transverse mounted horizontally opposed air-cooled twin cylinder 998 cc engine, the Rover Eight of the immediate post-Great War period has been likened to the current 2 CV Citroen, and it is interesting to speculate whether it would have soldiered on indefinitely had the Austin Seven not put in appearance in 1922. Like the oil-cooled Belsize-Bradshaw, "missing link" between the cyclecar and the light car, it was designed by J. Y. Sangster (of Ariel motorcycle fame) and boasted a three speed in-unit gearbox with shaft drive to a worm back axle. Lurid stories of cylinder heads glowing "cherry red" in the dark are so much fiction, but 17,000 found buyers up until 1925.

Although, generally speaking, American cyclecars tended to be larger engined and more substantial than their European counterparts, and the cyclecar craze tailed off more quickly following American entry into the war in 1917, there were exceptions. Few have not heard of Briggs & Stratton of Milwaukee, whose motor lawn mowers are still widely bought, and we may wonder at their survival when contemplating the 1919 Briggs & Stratton Flyer! The motorised wheel, which could be raised or lowered on a hinge to give traction(!), was built under licence to A.O. Smith of Milwaukee and was also made as the Wall Autowheel by B.S.A. in Britain.

A certain amount of mystery surrounds the Auto Red Bug electric roadster offered by Automotive Electrical Service Co. and Standard Autobile Corpn. of New Jersey between 1924 and 1928. In fact, it was an electric version of the Briggs & Stratton Flyer, a 12 volt battery driving the nearside rear wheel. According to Motor Wheeling Magazine, some enterprising Palm Beach dealers convinced local hotel owners that it would be fun to organise races for guests in the gardens of the hotels. These were popular for a couple of years, and the car was advertised as "the car which made Palm Beach famous"!

Patented by F. J. Camm, A.F.Ae.S. (better known as the founder-editor of The Practical Motorist *magazine*) and G.A. Broomfield, from whom it took its name, the diminutive Cambro has been likened to a child's pedal car and a flying roller skate, and certainly its specification was scarcely more complicated than either. Powered by rear mounted Johnson two stroke horizontally opposed twin (also called an Economic and used in the cyclecar of that name) it drove direct to the rear wheel by chain, having no gears but with a free wheel device to assist manhandling. Priced at £82 19s. 0d. it was built by Central Aircraft Co. of Kilburn in 1920 only.

In Germany during the twenties small cars proliferated, and well proven designs like the Austin Seven sold well there. Initially built under licence as the Dixi 3/15PS at Eisenach (as seen here) B.M.W. took over when they acquired Dixi, and when this arrangement ceased circa 1933 a complicated selling agreement was entered into between Longbridge and the Berlin branch of Willys Overland Crossley to market British-assembled left hand drive models in Germany. This continued until the outbreak of war and long after the parent Willys Overland Crossley company had been liquidated in Britain. The Dixi is seen here in a family group with a Model A Ford and a Tatra Type II.

The Cotay (or Co-tay – it was advertised under both names) was built in New York by Coffyn-Taylor Motor Co. (an unfortunate appelation) from 1920 until 1921 and sold in Britain by Bramco Ltd., of Coventry, at the inflated price of £470. The aircooled American Cameron four cylinder engine was used, Cameron being a member of the company, together with a centrally controlled three speed gearbox and conventional shaft drive. Even in inflation-ridden Britain in 1920 such a specification compared poorly with other British light cars and cyclecars and this is one of the few sold here.

Three wheeled cyclecars were scarcely more popular in France than in Britain although the Morgan was made under licence there by both Sandford and Darmont. One home-grown species which did quite well, however, was the D'Yrsan built by Raymond Siran of Cyclecars D'Yrsan at Asnières. Heavier than the Morgan and fitted with four cylinder Ruby engine, three speeds and shaft drive, it could, nonetheless, in sports form, exceed 80 mph. Although the make persisted from 1923 until 1930, three wheelers were made only until 1928. This is a 1925 model.

Current from 1911 until (in modified form) 1922, the first Wanderer was never a cyclecar in the true sense of the word, but like the Peugeot Quadrilette, also current during the early twenties, it employed tandem seating. Nicknamed the Püppchen (doll), it acquired a 1220 cc engine in 1914 and was eventually offered with three and four seater bodywork. Three forward speeds and shaft drive were enjoyed throughout the model's lifespan, and there were similarities with Adler's Model K.

Although the general layout is similar, and the name virtually the same, there was no connection whatever between the Wall tricar and the Leipzig-built Walmobil illustrated here. The giant and seven league boots are typical of the Wagnerian style of German advertising in 1920 when the Walmobil made its brief appearance. Power was provided by a twin cylinder 3/7PS engine mounted Phänomobil-style above the single chain driven front wheel.

Although D.K.W.'s first car was not announced until the 1928 Leipzig Fair, J.S. Rasmussen's Zschopauer Motoren-Werke was well known at Berlin Spandau for its two stroke motorcycles, and this 1927 three wheeled two stroke engined van was made in the motorcycle works. The car, when it appeared, was made in the old D-Rad motorcycle works which Rasmussen had taken over, and standardised a revolutionary chassis-less woodframed construction by Slaby (of Slaby-Beringer) allied to a 584 cc twin cylinder two stroke engine, latterly from 1931 with front wheel drive. It gained the nickname Das Kleine Wunder.

The versatility of the Phanomobil is amply illustrated in this photo taken in the Winter of 1916/17 in Sweden. The Swedish army officers are driving a four cylinder 1536 cc model of the type introduced in 1912, fitted with dual cooling fans and with skis substituted for the rear wheels. Production of this type continued with little alteration until 1927.

Like British aviation companies, those in
Germany found themselves with excess capacity
and no war contracts following the Armistice
and many turned to car and cyclecar production.
Grade of Bork bei Bruck were well known for
their aircraft, and when they produced their
Grade cyclecar it bristled with aviation features.
Of integral body/chassis construction, its
teardrop shape echoed Rumpler's larger
Tropfenwagen (rain drop car) and the car
enjoyed some competition success – particularly
at the Rennen Stadium. Engines were air-cooled
two stroke twins of 808 cc (980 cc in four seater
form) with chain final drive.

The little Hawa from Hanover was typical of the
small electric vehicles which proliferated in
Germany during the twenties and was built by a
manufacturer of railway rolling stock. As might
be expected from builders of railway carriages, a
coachbuilding section was also maintained, and
in addition to this pretty little coupé, they also
made a two seater and van, and supplied bodies
to Hanomag, Mauser and Apollo.

Moll-Werke of Chemnitz commenced production
with an orthodox light car which was also sold in
Britain by L.G. Hornsted as the Hornsted or the
Summers, but in 1924 Fritz Gorke designed for
them a tandem-seated boxy little vehicle which
was marketed under the name Mollmobil. A true
cyclecar, it was steered from the front seat and
was powered by D.K.W. engines of only 164 cc
and 198 cc and thence by exposed chain to the
solid rear axle.

So far as is known there was never a cyclecar hearse (although Bedelia supplied a field ambulance to the French army during the Great War). However, Dunkleys of Birmingham, the well known baby carriage makers (who also built some cars in 1896 and 1901 and the Matchless-engined Alvechurch cyclecar in 1911) offered this Pramotor in 1922. Cyclecarists were, therefore, catered for from the cradle, if not to the grave. Fitted with engines of 1hp and 2¼ hp they were expensive at 135 guineas and were forced by law to be used on the road only and not on the pavement.

It was not unusual for manufacturers to field the cars which they built in competitions, and here Charles Rouquet, pilots a Monitor built (circa 1920/21) in his Suresnes workshops on the Seine. The Monitor was powered by a 747 cc Vee-twin Train engine and was offered as either a front engined model with long belt drive or, as illustrated here, with rear mounted unit and chain drive running in an oil bath. This is a two seater, but a monocar was also available.

Robert O. Harper was originally Works Manager of Newton & Bennett, and designed the Anglo-Italian Newton-Bennett car and also the 1909 S.C.A.T., for which make his employers were sole U.K. concessionaires. The first Harper Runabout was built in his home workshop, but the design excited Sir William Letts of Crossley, who had acquired a controlling interest in aircraft manufacturers A. V. Roe Ltd. in 1920, and all production models were built by them. Resembling a three wheeled scooter and powered by a 269 cc Villiers two stroke, it was tougher and more practical than it looked, did well in the 1922 Scottish Six Day Trials and climbed the Brooklands test hill with a passenger! It was made until 1926.

Despite the popularity of electric vehicles in Germany during the 1920's, the 1922 Omnobil had a shorter life than most. Offered in two seater, four seater and light van form, and boasting 100 kilometres on a single charge, it was unfortunate in that it made its debut in the year in which the German mark collapsed. Its untimely demise may well have been due to this.

One of the few cyclecars built in Austria, the Austro-Rumpler from Vienna was made from 1920 until 1922 only as tiny single seater with 3/10 PS engine. Nevertheless, it sported the refinement of shaft drive to a live rear axle. The firm had no connection with Rumpler of Berlin, makers of the advanced Tropfenwagen.

As late as 1928, The Light Car & Cyclecar *was still advocating the single seat monocar, and actually went as far as to build this prototype Symons to illustrate its case. Powered by a Scott Flying Squirrel 498 cc watercooled two-stroke twin driving through a Scott three speed motorcycle gearbox and clutch, the Symons gave 70 mpg and was capable of over 50 mph, offered the comfort and weather protection of a saloon body with sunshine roof, ample luggage space and with the whole suspended on quarter elliptics all round. Nevertheless there were few takers.*

Chapter Four

Necessity is the Mother of Invention: The Thirties

The collapse of the American stock market on Wall Street in 1929 precipitated a World Trade Depression, the like of which had never before been seen, and which, with its far-reaching social and economic effects, is unlikely to be seen again. Many old and respected names in the established world of motor manufacture foundered during this period, which extended well into the Thirties, but like the London blitz it at least had the merit of sweeping away the bad as well as the good, leaving designers with a clean sheet upon which to plan anew.

Despite heavy unemployment and the Jarrow marchers, Britain of all the countries in the western world probably suffered least during this period, and as a result displayed a depressing lack of innovation in her light car designs. The Austin Seven soldiered on, little changed from its original 1922 specification, several motorcycle manufacturers essayed three wheelers – a trend which had commenced following the General Strike of 1926 – and Morgan, as ever, were in a class by themselves. Three wheelers enjoyed certain tax concessions, which kept them alive, but when these were swept away in the mid-Thirties, cars like the little J.A.P.-engined J.M.B., built in a moribund collar and cuff factory in the middle of the New Forest,

snuffed out virtually overnight.

France, where the small car had become entrenched in a big way during the Twenties, had become used to minimal devices like Charles Mochet's Velocar, and these appealed to the traditional frugality of the Gallic temperament – particularly in the provinces. Germany, its currency in tatters from 1922, and suffering from the ineffectual policies of the Weimar Republic, was totally wedded to cheap, small cars, however, and the cyclecar never really ceased to have a separate existence there. The brave new world promised by National Socialism and Hitler harnessed the talents of a whole galaxy of new designers, and Germany in the Thirties proved to be a forcing ground for all manner of innovative ideas on the automobile scene, even though its political policies were abhorrent in other departments.

America, being the biggest, fell the hardest, and yet the small car made little or no impact there during the Thirties. The American Austin (later Bantam) struggled financially throughout its existence, Hal Carpenter's Dart was stillborn, and the only successful small car – the Crosley – did not appear until the end of the decade. It was to take another war to bring back a revival of the minicar in the United States.

Alone among the original cyclecar builders, Morgan remained faithful to original concepts and first principles, and even the abolition of tax concessions for three wheelers in Britain during the thirties failed to daunt either the little Malvern-based company or the enthusiasts who drove their cars with such enjoyment. This 1935 Morgan Super Sports seen here taking part in the 1937 M.C.C. Torquay Rally is typical of the breed as it appeared during the depression-ridden thirties, although the bread-and-butter family model remained available, and the last three wheeler did not leave the factory until 1952.

Demonstrating the fact that the cyclecar owed no allegiance to any particular area, the Whitwood Monocar was built in Portsmouth, albeit by the well known Osborn Engineering Company, makers of the unorthodox O.E.C. motorcycle. Despite its title, the car was a tandem two seater similar in conception to the much earlier Mauser Einsperauto and employing only two wheels when moving. Powered by engines ranging from a 150 cc two stroke up to a 1000 cc J.A.P. Vee twin, this depression newcomer cost from £49 up to £85 and lasted from 1934 until 1936.

Better known for their bicycles and motorcycles, Raleigh of Nottingham made three separate attempts at the motorcar market. The first, in 1905, was a conventional four cylinder model, and this was followed in 1916 by a few cyclecars with two cylinder and four cylinder Alpha engines. Their 1922 flat twin was never marketed but 1933 Safety Seven shown here was built for three years. Designed by T. L. Williams, who subsequently bought the manufacturing rights and formed Reliant at Tamworth, it featured a 742 cc Vee twin engine, three speed gearbox and shaft drive and cost £110 5s.0d.

The depression years of the 1930's saw several motorcycle manufacturers essaying three and four semi-sports cars but the Coventry-Victor (unkindly nicknamed the "Country Vicar") was an older design dating from 1926 and it enjoyed a longer life than most. In 1933 "Midget" form as shown here, it differed little from the 1920's types and was extremely cheap at £75. Coventry-Victor's own 688 cc watercooled side valve flat twin provided the power, transmission being by chain.

One of the most successful of "packagers" in the 1930's, designer C. F. Beauvais, who had previously been responsible for the C.F.B. cyclecar, worked wonders with the ugly little Coventry-Victor three wheeler, and this 1932 "Luxury Sports" was the result. Fitted with a larger 749 cc version of the flat twin engine it was offered alongside the austere "Midget" and boasted a self starter and two tone paint job. Made until 1937, it gradually "grew up", acquiring progressively engines of 850 cc, 900 cc and finally 1000 cc. A 1949 prototype 747 cc flat four engined saloon – the Venus – was unfortunately stillborn.

Previously involved in the production of the Anglo-French (later totally British) Marlborough from 1909 until 1926, T. B. André, the shock absorber people, fielded the innovative André V6 between 1933 and 1934. Featuring independent front suspension by transverse leaf spring (an advanced design in Britain at the time), floor pan and chassis combined, the car developed 28 bhp at 4,500 rpm from a 728 cc overhead valve J.A.P. Vee twin engine, but only six cars were built in all. This one is shown at the Bugatti O.C. Amersham Hill Climb.

Jack Shillan was originally lessee of the Welsh Harp at Hendon and an enthusiastic advocate of small speed boats. As a logical progression from his "Scootaboat", his British Motor Boat Manufacturing Co. introduced in 1934 the Rytecraft Scootacar, primarily for use in fairgrounds and fun fairs, and Butlin's bought quite a few for their holiday camps. Powered by a 98 cc Villiers Midget industrial engine, and barred from Olympia by the S.M.M.T.(!), over 1500 were made, many being used for publicity purposes. This example was delivered in Paris three hours after it had been ordered, leaving Croydon airport at 12.30 pm on December 15th, 1934, in an Imperial Airways passenger Argosy!

This "Scootatruck" shared the same basic specification as the Scootacar although some versions were fitted with larger 2½ horsepower engines. Crowd stoppers, they were nevertheless used by a number of firms in truck and van form for carrying light loads, and customers included Slumberland, the bed people, and Morelands, who made the "England's Glory" safety matches.

Necessity being the "Mother of Invention", the otherwise forlorn years of the 1930's Depression were brightened by a galaxy of innovative designers, and whatever else may be said of Nazi Germany, nowhere else was this more true. Among the "heavyweights" – which included Ferdinand Porsche, Paul Henze, Fritz Fiedler and Paul Daimler – there existed a sub-strata of opinion, as it were, the chief spokesman for which was Josef Ganz, editor of Motor-Kritik and a staunch advocate of low cost motoring, small cars with tubular backbones, rear mounted air-cooled engines and all-round independent suspension – all the ingredients which subsequently emerged in Porsche's Volkswagen. This Ganz prototype was built for the Ardie motorcycle company of Nurenberg in 1930.

Ernst Neumann-Neander had been a body designer since before the Great War (and an artist before that) and in the early twenties his beautiful but bizarre bodies in mahogany and beaten copper characterised the Berlin-built Szawe cars. Between 1928 and 1939 he produced a number of cyclecars – most of them prototypes, like this 1930 example with 350 cc aircooled motorcycle engine mounted amidships on the offside. Another design – the Pionier – with engine mounted ahead of the front axle and driving the front wheels, tandem seating and independent suspension, appeared in 1934, but Neander, like Emile Claveau of Paris, was as Tim Nicholson has said, an experimenter in practice if not in intention, and few models achieved production status.

No one adhered so doggedly to the cyclecar principle, and for so long, as Charles Mochet. Commencing as just one of the myriad cyclecar constructors on the Seine in 1924, at which time his products were known under the name C.M., he marketed his last design as late as 1958, although there had been some gaps in between. His principal output, however, was devoted to the Velocar, an example of which is seen here outside the 1932 Paris Salon. Engineless and pedal propelled, it nevertheless sold steadily throughout the twenties and thirties and a 142 cc powered version was offered in 1929. Although the C.M. was a true cyclecar with 350 cc two stroke engine and chain drive, 1951 saw a return to minimal motoring with his CM125 Mochet, powered by a 125 cc Ydral engine. It required no driving licence in France!

Designed by Josef Ganz for Bungartz & Co. of Munich in 1934, the diminutive Butz seen here in chassis form, but outwardly resembling his later Standard Superior, bristled with advanced ideas. Featuring independent suspension by twin transverse leaf springs front and rear, and a rear mounted watercooled twin cylinder engine of 400 cc, its backbone type chassis was reminiscent of the later Volkswagen. A two wheeled trailer in matching colours accommodated the luggage!

Typical of the interesting designs which pervaded the German scene during the thirties (and which by 1939 had virtually banished traditional "cart" springing from the Fatherland) this sophisticated little car was home-built in 1931 by Gunther Wertheim of Berlin. It featured a central tubular frame, independent front suspension, a rigid back axle with cantilever springs mounted to the frame and incorporating a special layout of shock absorbers. The rear mounted single cylinder 500 cc engine drove the rear wheels by chain and the whole car weighed less than 400 kgs.

Prolific though he was, Josef Ganz succeeded in getting only one of his designs into what could truthfully be called series production. His Standard Superior, built at Ludwigsburg, was in fact licence-produced by Wilhelm Gutbrod (who built light cars under his own name at Plochingen between 1949 and 1954). Of aerodynamic appearance, it resembled his Butz, and followed his usual pattern of backbone frame, i.f.s., and a rear mounted twin cylinder two stroke engine of either 396 cc (shown here) or 494 cc. Production of cars continued from 1933 until 1935 but vans and station wagons were built until 1939. Below is the Standard Superior Sports.

The Czech Jawa took its name from the parent company Janecek of Prague and Wanderer after a licence had been acquired to produce Wanderer motorcycles. In 1934 another licence was taken out to build the D.K.W. car and the 1936 Jawa 700 shown here utilised the D.K.W. twin cylinder two stroke front wheel driving 684 cc engine and the chassis-less wooden framed body which characterised the D.K.W. Built on a slighter longer chassis than its alter ego, it was capable of 100 kph and was successful in many sporting events. It was replaced by a Tatra design in 1937.

Not to be confused with the Borgward-sponsored German Lloyd cars, the 1950 version of which featured a 293 cc twin cylinder engine, the British Lloyd hailed from Grimsby – about as unlikely a centre for motorcar manufacture as you are likely to find. Introduced in 1936 and as illustrated here, the earliest cars relied upon a rear mounted single cylinder 350 cc engine and their main customers seems to have been the Gas, Light & Coke Co., of Beckton, who used them for their inspectors. Fred Lloyd was an agent for Willys-Overland and Arrol-Johnston in the twenties and after the second war produced an advanced 650 cc vertical twin model with tubular back bone and i.f.s., the chassis of which can be seen in the background of this photo.

As well as the Ardie prototype, Josef Ganz also produced a design for Adler, of Frankfurt, in 1931 which, with all independently sprung wheels, backbone chassis and rear mounted engine, echoed a theme which he was destined to continue in various forms throughout the thirties. Named the "Maikäfer" (Maybug) and shown here, it was never produced, and when Adler announced a new model at the Geneva Show of 1932 it was to be the front wheel drive 1.5 litre Trumpf.

Because of the Nazi race laws Ganz, who was Jewish, was forced to flee to Switzerland in 1937, and whilst there he produced yet another cyclecar with tubular body frame and rear mounted M.A.G. (Motosacoche) 350cc single cylinder engine. The car, first known as the Erfiag, incorporated all Ganz's previously well-aired theories; after the second war Rapid Motormaher A.G. of Zurich were persuaded to lay down a batch of 36 under the Rapid name. They were unsuccessful, however, and Rapid resumed manufacture of motor mowers, scythes and light tractors.

From 1929 B.S.A., like several other British motorcycle firms, introduced a three wheeled sporting type light cyclecar. Nicknamed the "Beeza" it was based on the overhead valve 1100 cc Vee twin watercooled Hotchkiss engine originally made in 1921 to power the B.S.A. Ten made by the Birmingham Small Arms Co. of Sparkbrook. After Morris had taken over Hotchkiss in 1924, B.S.A. Cycles Ltd. of Small Heath purchased manufacturing rights in the engine and adapted it in 1 litre form to drive the front wheels of the "Beeza", which also boasted independent front suspension. This is a 1935 version which took first prize in the coachwork competition in the Torquay Rally. Note the knobbly trials tyres.

Despite the strictures of the Depression – 3,000 banks went to the wall in the United States – really small cars never caught on during the thirties, and even the licence-produced Austin Seven (American Austin – later Bantam) was unsuccessful. Powel Crosley, was a pioneer of radio manufacture, and his well made baby car succeeded in the climate of impending war when introduced in 1939. As shown here (1942) (with Paulette Goddard and Ray Milland) it utilised a 580 cc aircooled flat twin Waukesha engine, but acquired a four cylinder Cobra unit after the war.

Chapter Five

Vive l'Electrique: France and the Occupation

Whilst the Second World War effectively brought to a halt all civilian – and particularly private car – production, the uneasy months of the German Occupation of France brought some measure of peace to the inhabitants. The setting up of the Vichy Government, abhorrent though it may have been to the Free French fighting with the British forces as well as those domiciled in France, meant nevertheless a brief return to some form of normality. It is a measure of the fortitude and adaptability of the French nation that they should have, during this artificial period, actually embarked upon the manufacture of civilian vehicles – both private cars and light commercials.

Almost without exception, they were electrically powered, which is understandable in view of the almost total absence of fuel for civilian use, and among the newcomers were many old and respected names. Both Hispano-Suiza and Delaunay-Belleville essayed light

vans of the most primitive character, whilst Corre La Licorne offered electric versions of their 6CV and 7CV petrol types under the Aeric name, and Gendron, Duriez and Leyssieux would convert any suitable petrol-driven chassis to electricity for you.

In fact, at least twenty one separate establishments, including Georges Irat, Peugeot, C.G.E.-Tudor (J. A. Gregoire) and Breguet built battery-powered minicars and vans whilst France was under Nazi domination, and there were at least two in Holland.

Despite this activity, no great advances were made in the design of the electric, and with few exceptions it was conspicuous by its absence in the post-war austerity years, not only in France but everywhere. The difficulty of producing a battery light enough, small enough and sufficiently powerful to propel a small vehicle for a reasonable length of time on a single charge and at reasonable speed is a problem still engaging designers today.

The Le Dauphin was the brainchild of Parisian André L. Dauphin and, like the Mochet Velocar, was originally intended for pedal-power. 100 cc or 175 cc Zurcher two stroke engines were also available but a small electric motor was more popular. Steering from the rear seat, it reverted to the layout popularised by Bédélia thirty years before. Bodywork was by Kellner – oh! how the mighty have fallen.

It is a feature of the electrics which proliferated in Occupied France that many of them resembled superficially their cyclecar ancestors. There are shades of Marcel Violet's Sima-Violet about this c. 1942 Peugeot VLV electric – its single "Cyclops" headlamp echoing the exposed flywheel of the Violet-designed front mounted engine. No attempt was make by Peugeot to capitalise on any existing models during this period, and the VLV was an entirely new design and not an adaptation, as was the case, for instance, with the Aeric made by La Licorne. A two-seater cabiolet, the VLV was capable of 30 mph.

One of the better looking electrics built in France during the German Occupation, the C.G.E. Tudor was made by the Compagnie Generale Electrique in Paris from 1941 until 1946, and appeared at one post-war Salon with an optional closed coupé body. Production models were two seater cabriolets as illustrated here, with a cast aluminium frame designed by Jean Gregoire. With a maximum speed of 36 mph and a creditable range of 56 miles on one charge it compares favourably with modern electrics.

Chapter Six

Forever Blowing Bubbles: Post-War Austerity

Whilst it is fashionable to believe that the Suez crisis and the subsequent petrol rationing of 1956 was responsible for the boom in minicars after the War, the fact is that it merely added impetus to a trend which had become firmly established in the post-War austerity years – the "Stafford Cripps Era" – not only in Britain, but elsewhere all over the world. The Second World War was a "world" war in the true sense of the word, very few areas escaping unscathed, with the result that with a return to peace it was at least five years before the economic effects of a six year conflict (and the resulting shortages of raw materials) had even begun to be overcome.

The Paris Salon from 1946 onwards became renowned for its galaxy of outrageous minicars, and whilst only a fraction of these ever achieved production status, they indicated that the motoring public would welcome a device which would be kind to that precious book of petrol coupons, sufficiently low in price to avoid double purchase tax and so simple in its construction that it would not be so affected by material shortages as to demand a three-year waiting list.

As will be seen, a number of makers attempted to cater to this demand, but it was not until the advent of the Iso Isetta – and with it, the "bubble" craze – that the demand was really satisfied. The sudden growth of the minicar coincided, in fact – particularly in Britain – with the decline in popularity of the family motorcycle combination. The opportunity to have the whole family protected from the elements in a vehicle in which Mum could do the shopping and pick up the kids from school was one to be grabbed with both hands, and this defection by the family motorcyclists, allied to the bad publicity gained during the first rock 'n' roll Teddy Boy era, spelled the beginning of the end for the British motorcycle industry.

Just as Violet had flourished during the Twenties, and Ganz designs proliferated in the Thirties, so the Fifties provided their own prolific designers. Iconoclasts like Laurie Bond and Egon Brütsch assailed the old values vigorously, and during the free-for-all which followed Suez, something of the fun and the excitement of the first cyclecar era briefly returned.

Even the Americans thought seriously about small cars, although predictably they were larger than their European counterparts. The combined forces of Detroit had their way, however, and it was not until 1960 that any radical change of policy was to occur among the big battalions. When it came, the American "compact", although small by American standards, was a far cry from the minicar. It is significant, however, that it was prompted by the inroads made upon the American market by the Porsche-designed German Volkswagen – a vehicle which ironically inporated all the main ingredients advocated by minicar designer *par excellence* Josef Ganz during the Thirties.

Just as the Austin Seven had hastened the departure of the true cyclecar, it was to be another Austin Seven – the Issigonis Mini – which would revolutionise the small car world and eventually banish the "bubble" car to the pages of the history books. It appeared in 1959, has just completed its first successful twenty years, and looks like going on for some time yet. Its transverse-engined front wheel drive layout, radical when first announced, has now been adopted by virtually all the Mini's principal competitors. Yet, like the cyclecar, the Mini is beginning to grow up, and put on weight. With the final energy crisis only just around the corner, so we are told, is there not a strong case for a return to the concept of the original simple cyclecar – albeit allied to the benefits of modern technology and safety regulations? Certainly the French would seem to think so. Reference has previously been made to the traditional frugality of the French – which should not be confused with petty meanness—and which manifests itself as a "waste not, want not" no-nonsense down-to-earth philosophy which has enabled them to survive previous crises of a magnitude which would have finished any lesser nation.

It is, perhaps, typical, therefore that it should be they who have reacted in the most immediate – and sensible – manner to the world threat of an energy famine. 1979 witnessed growing unrest in Iran following the toppling of the Shah's regime, the uncertainty was exacerbated by the Russian intervention in Afghanistan. By the time that events such as these had begun to send their ripples through the world, however, France was well prepared. At least a dozen small regional companies were building – and selling in commendable numbers – an astonishing variety of mini-cars. In the originality of their design, the unorthodoxy of their operation and the spartan nature of their construction and appearance they are, perhaps, the nearest attempt we have seen since World War II to return to the concept of the simple cyclecar.

Naturally, they employ modern materials, and benefit from the rapid advances which have been made in the development of really small engines since the war. Thus most of them (like the creations of Mochet) require no driving licence under French law, are exceptionally cheap to insure, and are even in some cases exempt from the parking restrictions applicable to normal sized vehicles.

France was one of the last countries to support a regionally distributed motor industry, and it is interesting, therefore, that this new generation of cyclecars are also widely scattered throughout France and are therefore rarely seen outside the immediate district in which they are built. Doubtless, the limitations of a 49cc engine are responsible, and the cars are of the greatest use as shopping runabouts for mother and one (or perhaps two) small children in the congested urban streets. As in the days of the original cyclecar, however, it is the simplicity of construction and design which can support light industry.

It might be thought that America, with the particular problems which two and three car families face there in the wake of fuel restrictions allied to large engine capacities, might have taken the lead in the introduction of ultra-small cars for town and city use, but little appears to have been done. News has filtered out, however, of the Deluxe Free-Way 11, a mini three-wheeler powered by petrol, diesel or electric motor and priced at US$2295 (which seems expensive). It is built in Bloomington, Minnesota.

In fact, although it is only now that details of these fascinating little vehicles are becoming more generally known – they are appearing in increasing numbers on the French roads – several have been made for some years. The Arola, originally a three wheeler and now offered as a four wheeler as well, has been made in Lyon – erstwhile home of many illustrious French makes – since 1976. It is powered by a Sachs two-stroke of only 47cc, and is, therefore, typical of the type.

Mainly bodied in fibreglass, the permutations are, however, virtually endless. Engines are mainly of the two-stroke air-cooled motorcycle or moped variety, but two-stroke industrial diesels and electric motors are also employed allied to both front and rear wheel drive. The Villejuif-built Flipper rejoices in a system whereby the front-mounted Sachs 47cc engine and the two front wheels (which are of narrower track than those at the rear) pivot through 360° permitting a quite astonishing turning circle! Such idiosyncracies are not only extremely practical for urban operation, but entirely in keeping with the traditions of the true cyclecar.

There is a mounting revolt against the complications, expense, and rationalisations of life in the Seventies and Eighties. Already we have a return to real ale – might not a new cyclecar revolution also be brewing?

The Westfalia single seater was made in the mid-fifties by Fahrzeug-Fabrik H.W. Voltmann. A three wheeler with open bodywork and handlebar steering it was powered by a 125 cc Ilo two stroke engine with self starter. Designated the M 50 it was popular – as were many cyclecars – with invalids.

Although several of the post-second war "bubble" cars had front opening doors, Wilhelm Meyer's Meyra 200 was unusual in that only half the front of the vehicle actually opened. A three wheeler, with wheel steering, fully enclosed cabin and sliding windows, it was chain driven by a single cylinder 197 cc Ilo two stroke to the single rear wheel. About 50 of this model were made, between October 1953 and April 1955.

Originator's of the mid-fifties "Bubble" look, Iso's little Isetta was introduced in 1953 and managed only three full seasons in its native Italy. Doubtless the competition provided by Fiat's Topolino and the motorcycle industry combined to force it out, but that was not the end of the story. Licence-produced by B.M.W. in Germany (the most successful producer), in Britain and in France, the final total was some 36,000 units. Flagrantly imitated by Hoffman in Germany – the court action put them out of business – the design relied upon a rear mounted 236 cc two stroke twin with common combustion head and a front opening door. This example is competing in the 1955 Mille Miglia.

Like Marcel Violet in the twenties, and Josef Ganz in the thirties, Laurie Bond's post-second war designs cropped up in various guises and with different sponsors. The first and most successful of these was the Lancashire-built Bond Minicar introduced in 1948 and, as the Bond Bug, in production up to 1975. Initially powered by a 122 cc (later 197 cc) two stroke Villiers mounted over the single chain driven front wheel, the Bond employed a 3 speed motorcycle gearbox and unitary body/chassis construction totally unsprung at the rear.

By 1954 the Bond was well established, had acquired separate front wings, a glass (rather than perspex) windscreen, optional electric starter, front wheel brakes and bonded rubber rear suspension. Four seater versions were available from the same year onwards and Lt. Col. Michael Crosby (left) and co-driver Captain T. Mills, seen here at Lympne airport, participated (unofficially) in the Monte Carlo Rally in the example illustrated.

From 1954 onwards Bond made increasing use of fibreglass to replace the original aluminium bodywork and a 246 cc four speed version, still with Villiers engine, was announced in 1959, and standardised in 1960. The Minicar persisted up to 1965 but then acquired Hillman Imp mechanics and continued in this guise until 1969. Reliant of Tamworth then bought the company, transferred production from Preston, and concentrated on the Bug, powered by Reliant's own 700 cc (later 750 cc) o.h.v. engine as illustrated here in this 1970 version.

Even the most ardent advocates of the minicar are bound to admit that the Peel, and particularly the single seater P50 model, was little more than a chair in a box with wheels. The Trident, a slightly larger version made in 1965, used the same 49 cc Auto Union single two stroke driving the single rear wheel and with brightly coloured fibreglass body and one-piece perspex moulding roof earned itself the nickname of the "clockwork orange" or the "crash helmet". It was made in the Isle of Man.

Ernst Heinkel's Cabin Cruiser was perhaps better looking than the Isetta and although it sold a mere 6,000 units in its native Germany, it too was built under licence in Britain and elsewhere. With a front-opening door it resembled the Isetta in appearance, however, although the 174 cc Heinkel engine was somewhat smaller. Trojan of Croydon – certainly no strangers to unorthodoxy – took out a licence in Britain and even produced a light van version, prolonging its life until 1965.

Hairiest of the "bubbles" was Willi Messerschmitt's Tiger, illustrated here. Resembling the cockpit of one of his wartime Me109's, its 500 cc Sachs twin cylinder engine was capable of propelling it indecently fast, although earlier three wheeled models were powered by 175 cc and 200 cc Sachs units. It was developed from a design by Fritz Rosenheim for a cheap invalid carriage for disabled ex-servicemen and in this respect echoed the peculiar tandem seated 1919 Landini cyclecar which featured rudder bar control and foot steering, being designed by a flying instructor for disabled flyers.

Not only Messerschmitt, but Heinkel and Dornier (all three wartime aircraft manufacturers in Germany) involved themselves with the "bubble" car boom, although Claude Dornier's son's design was sold as the "Delta" to Zundapp, who renamed it the Janus. Squarer in shape than either the Heinkel or the Isetta, it carried a 248 cc two stroke engine amidships between two sets of seats which faced backwards and forwards respectively. This arrangement necessitated doors at both front and back of the vehicle, which took its name from the Roman god who faced both ways.

Coincidentally, a wartime career in aviation was the background of the sponsor of the unpromising little Faithorpe Atom from Chalfont St. Peter, Bucks. (later Gerrard's Cross and Denham) announced in 1954. A fibreglass two/four seater with independent suspension and rear mounted B.S.A. engines ranging from 250cc to 650cc, it was designed by wartime Mosquito pilot Air Vice-Marshal D.C.T. "Pathfinder" Bennett. Faster than most minicars, it was crudely finished but quickly developed into a fully fledged conventional front engined sports car.

The C.H.S., designed and built by the Asnières-based Chausson bus company in 1948, deserved a better fate. Featuring a single cylinder watercooled two stroke engine of only 330cc which drove the front wheels, and rear mounted radiator, it boasted all independent suspension and an attractive, light, open two seater body. The example shown here was photographed outside the premises of L.T. Delaney & Sons, of Cricklewood, who tried to interest Austin in making it in England. However, Austin could not get the necessary allocation of steel, and the project was dropped.

John and Charles Cooper's Surbiton-based (later Byfleet) company is best remembered for the 500cc single seater racing cars (in which Stirling Moss cut his racing teeth) built from 1948 onwards, and the later successful Formula 1 and Formula 2 racers and BMC Mini Cooper Specials. Earlier still, however, in 1947 a few J.A.P.-engined sports cars were built and one is illustrated here.

Said to have been financed from the profits from football pools, the 1954 Vernon seen here in prototype form achieved production status at Bidston in Cheshire as the Gordon. Judging by the road test reports in the contemporary press, its specification set no one's passions on fire and it really was a rather ugly little vehicle. A three wheeler, it carried its 197cc Villiers engine in a bulge-cum-air-scoop on the offside amidships, whence it drove one rear wheel by chain. Its chief virtue appears to have been its low price of £300 and it lasted until 1958.

Lineal descendent of the original A.C. Sociable, the Petite, introduced at Thames Ditton in 1953 did not, unfortunately share the success of its ancestor. Its rear mounted 350cc Villiers engine tended to overheat and become noisy with use, and for a period A.C. (who had also made 250cc B.S.A. engined invalid cars) laboured under the back handed compliment that they made the fastest and the slowest cars in the land.

S.E. Opperman of Borehamwood were best known for their J.A.P. engined three wheeled goods carrier, the Motocart, but in 1956 they commissioned Laurie Bond to design a minicar. The resulting Unicar – an angular fibreglass creation with ill-fitting doors was offered at under £400 with a choice of Excelsior 225cc or British Anzani 328cc engines mounted at the rear. In the latter form the car was good for 75 mph while 85 mpg was claimed for the smaller engine. Offered in kit form with hire purchase by Bowmaker Ltd., a sports version – the Stirling with Steyr-Puch 500 engine was announced at Earls Court in 1958 but at almost £500 it was too expensive and few sold.

Laurie Bond's other sports car – the Berkeley built for Charles Panter's caravan group at Biggleswade – met with more success when announced in 1956. Using the same British Anzani engine as the Unicar (later a 328 cc Excelsior twin) and with bolted up fibreglass bodywork, the car was good for 65 mph and looked attractive into the bargain. These are part of a batch that went to California. The marque enjoyed some competition success, winning its class in the 1959 Mille Miglia and the Monza 12 Hour Race, defeating several streamlined Fiat-Abarths in the process. An unsuccessful three wheeler hastened the Berkeley's demise in 1960.

Very few electric cars were ever built in Britain – unlike Germany and France where, over the years, they proliferated. A late example introduced in 1952 and produced in Hove, Sussex, of all places, was the B.M.A. Hazelcar which took its name from R.E. Hazeldine of Hazeldene Motors, Telscombe Cliffs. Built by Gates & Pearson in Alice Street, it featured an angular aluminium body, small scooter-like wheels and a 1½ hp electric motor driving a double reduction Duplex chain. Giving 18-20 mph with a range of 50-60 miles it was expensive at £535 and a van version tempted no one.

Despite sorties into the cyclecar world between 1913 and 1922 and again in 1932, Douglas of Bristol remained wedded to their horizontally-opposed twin motorcycles and never again essayed car production. A locally built sports car, the Clifton-based Iota, did however employ the Douglas 350 cc flat twin engine, allied to a four speed gearbox and chain final drive. The Iota was introduced experimentally in 1951 by a small specialist racing car firm better known for their "500"s. An impressive 70 mph and 70 mpg were claimed but production never commenced.

On a par with Violet, Bond, and Ganz was perhaps the ebullient Egon Brütsch, Europe's most persistent purveyor of unorthodoxy in the post-war period. Basically German, his confections popped up endowed with different names and different nationalities. All were derived from the Zwerg (dwarf), a monocoque three wheeler with tubular framing, rubber suspension and 65 mph from 200cc, and included the 50cc Mopetta, and the four wheeled Pfeil. The latter was sponsored by both the Bavarian Spatz concern and the Victoria motorcycle company. With tubular backbone and 200cc Sachs (later 248cc Victoria) engine, about 1500 found buyers.

Whilst it may have progressed beyond the motorised bath chair, the Larmar invalid carriage from Ingatestone in Essex, built between 1946 and 1951, was an uncompromisingly ugly little beast, albeit it enjoyed the luxury of a single "Cyclops" headlamp, windscreen and disappearing hood. A four wheeler, its 250cc engine was mounted at the rear and totally enclosed and driven by single chain to one rear wheel. With a cruising speed of 30-35 mph (and exempt from purchase tax for invalids) it cost £198.

In business from 1950 until 1962, W.R. Pashley Ltd. of Birmingham concentrated on tri-vans – until 1954 a single model with 197 cc Villiers engine and 3 cwt (later 4 cwt) carrying capacity. A later 10 cwt version with 600 cc engine was theoretically available also as a "motor rickshaw" but the 197 cc minicar introduced in 1953 and illustrated in prototype form here was unsuccessful. At £265 it undercut the Bond by £4.

It is perhaps inevitable that an iconoclast like Philip Vincent should have been drawn, albeit briefly, into the world of the minicar. When, in the 1950's, sales of his superbikes began to decline and extreme excursions into the economy class with the 48 cc Firefly failed to restore the firm's fortunes, the Stevenage works experimented with an attractive three wheeled sports two seater fitted with a Vee twin Vincent 1000 cc engine driving the rear wheel by chain. Although its performance must have been interesting, it did not achieve series production.

The emergence of Robert de Rovin's rear engined minicar in 1946 from St. Denis, the erstwhile home of Delaunay-Belleville – once considered the Gallic Rolls-Royce – was not so illogical as it may seem, since Delaunay-Belleville themselves built some electric powered economy cars during the German Occupation. Raoul de Rovin had built cyclecars during the twenties, but not for sale, and his brother's products were in any event neat advanced little cars with backbone chassis, chain-cum-shaft drive and three speed synchromesh gear boxes. Production models initially used a side valve aircooled single cylinder engine of 260 cc. This is the later model with watercooled flat twin 425 cc engine, introduced in 1948 and made until 1959.

The 1953 Eshelman Sportabout from Baltimore was, together with the Athens, Ohio-built King Midget, one of the survivors of a post second war flurry (one could not call it a boom) in minicars in the United States. Mainly aimed at the golf club fraternity and as a shopping runabout it claimed 30 mph and 50 mpg from its 8.4 hp aircooled engine. One questions the logic of an optional snow plough attachment(!) but in any event only 16 units were completed. King Midget, with 9¼ hp Kohler engine, managed to turn out 5,000 cars between 1946 and 1969.

Although Reliant's Tamworth works were established by designer T. L. Williams in 1935, the first car model – the Regal – did not appear until 1952. Up until then the company had concentrated upon vans, from 1939 fitted with a modified Austin Seven engine built in the works. Undoubtedly the most successful of the post-war three wheelers, and probably the most refined, Reliants retained the Austin-based engine until 1963, replacing this with their own die cast 600 cc o.h.v. unit. Over 50,000 of this model had been sold by April 1968.

Like Reliant's four wheeled Rebel, later versions of the three wheeler, such as this 1957 model, were bodied in fibreglass, acquiring engines of 700 cc (also fitted to the four wheeled Rebel) in 1970. Following the acquisition of Bond in 1969 Reliant became the second largest all-British producer, with an annual output (including four wheelers) of 20,000 plus. The Regal's engine size was increased to 748 cc in 1973 and this unit was shared with the Bond Bug. In 1981 the three wheeler is still going strong, now represented by the 848 cc Robin and Super Robin, the Bug having been dropped after the 1975 model year.

It would probably be true to say that the Reliant Robin represents the last true cyclecar built in Britain – at the time of going to press at least. At one time part of banker Julian Hodge's empire, Reliant of Tamworth have weathered the vicissitudes of the post-war market, and in many ways resemble A.C., whose Petite and Cobra models represented the opposite ends of the spectrum. Whilst their Scimitar G.T.E. caters for the young executive, the Robin appeals to the same family man who up until the mid-fifties would have bought a motorcycle combination or a small pre-war saloon. Fitted with the four cylinder 848 cc engine designed by Reliant themselves, and with fibreglass bodywork, the cheapest version cost £2,875 in 1981 and in Super Robin form, £3,325. A far cry from the pre-war Austin Seven-based vans.

Wholly British, the Scootacar (no connection with the pre-war Rytecraft) bubble car was more correctly described as a cabin scooter and was built in Leeds from 1957 until (unusually late) 1964. In de luxe form, represented as a three seater (two would have been a squeeze), it offered only one door on the nearside and was powered by a 197 cc (later 346 cc) Villiers engine. Discomfort and a high centre of gravity were offset by £5 road tax and running cost (pre-decimal) of 1¼d. per mile.

Quite why the German Fuldamobil should have been so popular is something of a mystery but in one guise or another it enjoyed a twenty year production run between 1950 and 1970. Offered as a three wheeler, initially with alloy panelling on a wood frame and subsequently with all steel and finally fibre glass bodywork, it was available at first with both 250 cc Ilo and 360 cc Sachs engine, but a 200 cc Ilo was later standardised. In Britain it was made as the Nobel 200 for York Nobel Industries by Harland & Wolfe of Belfast and (abortively) by Lea-Francis. Two versions are illustrated, a 1953 Fuldamobil N-2 and a 1960 Nobel 200, but the car was also made in India, Chile, and Greece.

Designed by the Italian Piaggio aircraft company (who were also responsible for the Douglas-built Vespa scooter), the Vespa 400 minicar was built by A.C.M.A. in Fourchamboult in France. More refined than most, it featured a sunshine roof, two opening doors, rear mounted vertical twin aircooled two stroke 400 cc engine and three speed synchromesh gearbox. Add to this all round independent suspension and the Vespa was really in the Fiat 500 and Bianchina class.

The Dingolfing firm of Hans Glas had been long established in the manufacture of agricultural machinery when, in 1955, they introduced their tiny Goggomobil. Taking its name from a German-designed scooter, the Goggo, built in 1951, the car was offered initially with 250 cc, 300 cc (as illustrated) and 400 cc two cylinder rear-mounted two stroke engines. Later on these were exchanged for front mounted 600 cc and 700 cc two cylinder four strokes, and when the Goggomobil was finally withdrawn in 1966, over 250,000 had been built.

The Spanish economy took a long time to recover from the ravages of the Civil War, and there was no serious manufacture of medium-sized cars until the arrival of the Fiat-sponsored SEAT in 1953. With few imported cars either, the field was clear for a multitude of minicar makers to try their luck, and there were at least a dozen offering their wares between 1950 and the early sixties. Best known was the Barcelona-built Biscuter which had been designed by the great Gabriel Voisin, builder of French luxury cars between the wars. It was powered by a 197cc Hispano-Villiers two stroke engine which drove the front wheels, and most were made in this spartan two seater form, although there was also a fibreglass coupé version known as the Plastico 200, and commercial models. About 5,000 Biscuters were made between 1951 and 1958.

The Biscuter's closest rival in sales was the P.T.V., also made in Barcelona, but with a more sophisticated specification which included hydraulic brakes, independent suspension all round and a 250cc Ausa two cylinder engine mounted at the rear in unit with a three speed transaxle. About 1,250 were made from 1956 to 1962.

A late arrival on the Spanish scene was the Clua, made by a motorcycle manufacturer from 1958 to 1960. With a fibreglass body and a 497cc two cylinder four stroke engine, it should have had a reasonable performance to complement its sporty looks.

Quite unsporting are the last two of our Spanish selection, the Isetta-like Triver (above) and the David three wheeler (below). The Hispano-Villiers powered Triver had its two rear wheels mounted close together in the manner of the 1920 Merrall-Brown; only a few were made, in the early 1950s. The David had a long ancestry, for it came from the same company which had made belt-driven cyclecars from 1913 to 1922 (see page 66), and also a few electric cars during the Civil War. An unusual variant on the 346 cc single cylinder cabriolet illustrated was a five wheeled commercial version.

Despite its Alfa Romeo-like radiator grille it is unlikely that the Milanese Volpe fooled anyone, and indeed its 125cc engine was one of the smallest fitted to any postwar minicar. With a streamlined open two seater body, however, which was quite advanced for 1947, and a four speed pedal-controlled preselective gearbox, the Volpe was no sluggard. Its diminutive twin cylinder two stroke developed 6bhp at 5,000 rpm and propelled it at a commendable 47 mph.

The diminutive P. Vallee built by the Societe Colas at Loir-et-Cher between 1952 and 1957 was powered by a 125cc engine (a Ydral) which obviated the necessity – in its native France – for a driving licence. Rubber suspension was employed, and in 1957 a new model offering 125cc and 175cc engines was marketed under the name Chantecler (Cockerel) presumably after the cock featured on the radiator badge. This example was shown at the 1952 Paris Salon.

The Czech firm of Velorex were better known for their motorcycles until 1958 when this tubular framed three wheeler was introduced. An unusual feature is the imitation leather bonnet and rear body panels affixed with press studs over the tubular frame. Powered with 250 cc or 350 cc Jawa engines it was current until 1971; a four wheeled version with 350 cc engine appeared in 1972.

Originally announced as the Jarc, the Astra was so-christened by its new sponsors, British Anzani of Hampton Hill in Middlesex. Current from 1956 until 1959 and originally powered by a 250 cc Excelsior Talisman twin two stroke it, logically, acquired the Anzani 322 cc unit following the take-over. A two-seater coupe version was marketed by a separate company as the Gill Getabout in 1958, but this rear engined model (which had been intended, in four seater form, for taxi work) was unsuccessful.

One of the fascinating aspects of the ultra-light cyclecar and micro-car is that they can be (and are) built by virtually any company. Activities as diverse as stage lighting and washing machine manufacture have, from time to time provided the finance and the manufacturing facilities for them. Not unnaturally the retail motor trade is well represented, but in the case of the Minnow built from 1951 until 1952 by Bonallack & Son of Forest Gate, London E.7 a background of commercial vehicle bodybuilding certainly helped. A three wheeler, powered by a 250 cc Excelsior Talisman twin cylinder two-stroke driving the single rear wheel, with auxiliary cooling scoops aft of the doors, the Minnow was distinguished by a single centrally mounted headlamp and could return 70 mpg at 45 mph.

Although they have at last fallen from favour and are giving way to BL Minis with special hand controls, it is probably true to say that the invalid carriage even in its 1970's form represented the last true manifestation of the cyclecar — as opposed to the minicar. This 1959 rear engined Tippen Delta is typical of the post-war breed.

One of the most endearing and idiosyncratic of the "new wave" of French cyclecars, the Villejuif-built Flipper relies upon a fibreglass monocoque construction moulded initially in two halves and bonded together to give a rigid construction. Such refinements as independent suspension of all four wheels by McPherson strut and telescopic damper and fully enclosed two seater bodywork are allied to a unique front wheel drive system which dictates that both front wheels and engine – a single cylinder 49cc Sachs two stroke – pivot from a central mounting through 360° giving a turning circle akin to that of a fairground dodg'em car.

This example is illustrating its extraordinary parking abilities between a Renault and a Silver Shadow.

A number of minicars were made in Latin America in the 1960s, including the Rago from Montevideo, Uruguay. Launched in 1967 by the brothers Waldemar and Carlos Rago, it had a rear-mounted Hispano-Villiers 325 cc 2-stroke engine with integral three-speed gearbox, and two-passenger fibreglass body. Top speed was said to be an effortless 45 mph. No more than twelve Ragos were made and sold as within a few months the Rago brothers decided that it was not worthwhile continuing production, and opted to make only fibreglass components for motorcycles and cars. A few Ragos are still in daily use in Uruguay.

Hailing from Saint-Barthelemy-d'Anjou, the Super Comtesse follows the general pattern of modern French cyclecar, albeit the 49 cc engine is by Motobecane rather than Sachs. Bodywork is a boxy design (rather reminiscent of Doctor Who's Daleks) of stratified polyester on a tubular frame accommodating two adults and reasonable luggage. Offered in ivory or orange (!), it boasts the refinement of automatic transmission and electric starting, tilting seats to give access to the luggage space, parcel rack, and coil spring suspension with dampers. The Bel-Motors Veloto C10 from Les Sables d'Olonne also favours the Motobecane unit, polyester bodywork, and electric starting, but features a novel rubber suspension.

Most prolific of all the modern cyclecar producers, at least in terms of multiplicity of models, the Paris-based Vitrex Industries are currently offering the Riboud convertible with either three or four wheels, (above) as the Marina, the Gildax (below) – a hard top coupé with doors and the choice of three or four wheels, the Snuggy Tobrouk and Snuggy Export three wheelers (both with Italian Morini 49 cc engines, as opposed to the Sachs 47 cc employed on the other models) and the diminutive Tri-50, a tubular framed delivery tricycle with rudimentary protection for the driver and chain driven rear wheel.

Index